on track ...

REO Speedwagon

every album, every song

James Romag

SONIC**BOND**

sonicbondpublishing.com

Sonicbond Publishing Limited
www.sonicbondpublishing.co.uk
Email: info@sonicbondpublishing.co.uk

First Published in the United Kingdom 2023
First Published in the United States 2023

British Library Cataloguing in Publication Data:
A Catalogue record for this book is available from the British Library

Copyright James Romag 2023

ISBN 978-1-78952-262-4

Typeset in ITC Garamond Std & ITC Avant Garde Gothic Pro
Printed and bound in England

Graphic design and typesetting: Full Moon Media

Special thanks to

Sara Romag, Heather Bigeck, Eric Boulanger, Carole Carter (Carolyn Conroy), Nancy Claar Flom, Richard Galbraith, Marvin Gleicher, Ted Habeck, Michael Jahnz, Anne Keuler, Stephen Lambe, Graham Lear, Terry Luttrell, Steven Mertes, Jennifer Nanzer, Lida Philbin, Ron Romero, Steve Scorfina, Jimmy Scott, Marty Shepard, Kathleen Sullivan, Greg X. Volz, Art Weiss, Arnie White (Naldo Sterling), and everyone who's ever been part of the REO family.

Would you like to write for Sonicbond Publishing?

At Sonicbond Publishing, we are always on the lookout for authors, particularly for our two main series. At the moment, we only accept books on music-related subjects.

On Track. Mixing fact with in-depth analysis, the On Track series examines the work of a particular musical artist or group. All genres are considered, from easy listening and jazz to 60s soul to 90s pop, via rock and metal.

Decades. An in-depth look at an important calendar decade in the career of a well-known artist or group.

While professional writing experience would, of course, be an advantage, the most important qualification is to have real enthusiasm and knowledge of your subject. First-time authors are welcomed, but the ability to write well in English is essential.

Sonicbond Publishing has distribution throughout Europe, North America and Australia and all books will also published in E-book form. Authors will be paid a royalty based on sales.

Further details are available from www.sonicbondpublishing.co.uk.

To get in touch, complete the contact form there or email info@sonicbondpublishing.co.uk

Follow us on social media:
Twitter: https://twitter.com/SonicbondP
Instagram: https://www.instagram.com/sonicbondpublishing_/
Facebook: https://www.facebook.com/SonicbondPublishing/

Linktree QR code:

on track ...

REO Speedwagon

Contents

A Man Walks into a Classroom (The Origins of REO Speedwagon)...............6
R.E.O. Speedwagon (1971)..14
R.E.O./T.W.O. (1972) 20
Ridin' the Storm Out (1973) 25
Lost in a Dream (1974)...31
This Time We Mean It (1975) 35
R·E·O (1976)...40
Live – You Get What You Play For (1977)...44
You Can Tune a Piano, but You Can't Tuna Fish (1978) 47
Nine Lives (1979)..54
A Decade of Rock and Roll 1970 to 1980 (1980) 60
Hi Infidelity (1980) 63
Good Trouble (1982) 72
Wheels are Turnin' (1984) 78
Life as We Know It (1987)..86
The Hits (1988)...92
The Earth, a Small Man, His Dog and a Chicken (1990)...........................96
The Second Decade of Rock and Roll 1981 to 1991 (1991).....................103
Building the Bridge (1996)..105
The Ballads (1999)...112
Arch Allies: Live at Riverport (2000) 115
Find Your Own Way Home (2007)...117
Not So Silent Night – Christmas with REO Speedwagon (2009)..................123
Live at Moondance Jam (2013)..131
Can't Stop Rockin' – REO On the Road from 2013 133
Additional Compilations and Live Releases 141
References 143

A Man Walks into a Classroom (The Origins of REO Speedwagon)

The REO Motor Car Company and its Speed Wagon might be little remembered by other than automotive enthusiasts, were it not for that fateful autumn day in 1967 at the University of Illinois at Champaign. That was when Neal Doughty walked into his History of Transportation class and there, on the blackboard at the front of the classroom for any aspiring musician in need of a band name, were the words 'REO Speed Wagon.' Keyboardist Doughty and bandmate Alan Gratzer would take that name to incredible heights over the following decades, forging a band that, more than 50 years later, is still going strong.

Gratzer had been playing drums and perfecting his craft in bands like The High Numbers and The Barbarians since high school and was studying aeronautical engineering at Champaign, about 150 miles southwest of Chicago. He'd been performing at various joints in central Illinois and around 1965, The High Numbers released a self-financed single ('I'm a Man'/'High Heel Sneakers') on their own Ocean label. Doughty had just started his studies in electrical engineering in the fall of 1966 when, on his first night at the university, he met Gratzer. That very night they jammed in the basement of their dormitory, the Illinois Street Residence Hall. Doughty, who'd taken trumpet lessons as a child and was part of his high school marching band, had taught himself to play his parents' piano. He often attended Gratzer's shows over the 1966-1967 school year and occasionally sat in with the band.

Around May 1967, as the school year drew to a close, Gratzer, bassist Mike 'Smokey' Blair, and guitarist Joe Matt were ready to start a different band that would include Doughty on keyboards. The members of the newly formed combo went their separate ways over the summer. They regrouped as planned in the fall and immediately started rehearsing. At this point, the yet-unnamed band was a four-piece: Gratzer on drums and vocals, Doughty on keyboards, Blair on bass and some vocals, and Matt on guitar and vocals. It was Doughty's first official band.

They were now a proper musical group, but to secure gigs they needed a name. The same day in 1967, they decided to find a name was the day Doughty spotted 'REO Speed Wagon' on his classroom blackboard. The vehicle was a marvel in its day, a flatbed delivery truck boasting an unusual combination of speed and power (perfect for use as a fire truck, among other things), which fit the fledgling band's intentions. The band made Speed Wagon into one word (which even the motor company sometimes did) and decided to use the separate initials R.E.O., rather than pronouncing it ree-oh, the way the motor company did.

As for the original vehicle, the REO Speed Wagon was named after its creator, automobile industrialist Ransom Eli Olds, who had previously been responsible for the Oldsmobile. In 1904, Olds departed Olds Motor Works after numerous disputes with his son, and founded the R.E. Olds Motor Car

Company (later REO Motor Car Company). Various models of the Speed Wagon were produced from about 1915 until the 1950s. The well-known logo for the band is based on the vehicle's logo of an encircled 'REO' with wings spread to the sides. Sometime in 1971, around the time of REO's first album release, General Motors authorized the band's use of the name and logo.

With the band name decided, the band soon played their first official gig under the Speedwagon moniker at a campus fraternity party. When they arrived, they found the walls where they were to play covered in brown paper for a planned food fight, a prank on the sorority that the fraternity had invited over. The show did indeed turn into a food fight, with the band scraping mashed potatoes out of Gratzer's drumkit the following day. More fraternity gigs followed, along with shows at other school-related events and local bars. One such bar where REO regularly played was Red Lion Inn in Champaign, which became a second home to the band. Additional often-played venues included Champaign's Illini Brown Jug and Chances R, along with The Morgue in Decatur.

Other bands playing the same circuit included One-Eyed Jacks and Feather Train (sometimes 'The Feather Train'). The ranks of One-Eyes Jacks included future REO members Michael Murphy and Bruce Hall, as well as future songwriting collaborator Tom Kelly. Feather Train, too, included future REO members, with both Bruce Hall and Gary Richrath passing through.

It was around this time that another university student, Irving Azoff (a mathematics and chemistry major), partnered with Bob Nutt. Their booking agency, Blytham, Ltd., handled dozens of local and regional acts, including Guild, One-Eyed Jacks, Lemon Pipers, Finchley Boys, Ohio Express, and REO. In short time, Azoff made the shift from booking acts to managing them. The first act he signed as a manager was REO Speedwagon.

Shortly after signing REO, Azoff took on singer/songwriter Dan Fogelberg, and, not long after, added The Eagles and later Steely Dan to his roster. Among other career highlights, Azoff was chairman of MCA Music Entertainment Group, started Giant Records at Warner Music Group, and coproduced such movies as *Fast Times at Ridgemont High*. In 2012 he was named the most powerful person in the music industry by US trade publication *Billboard*. In 2020 he was inducted into the Rock and Roll Hall of Fame in recognition of his life's work. It all started back in Illinois with local act REO.

In the early days, REO played soul and blues, but included what were then lesser-known covers, with The Doors' 'Light My Fire' (Doughty having mastered it on organ) frequently used as the closing number in their set. Since Gratzer sang about half of the band's setlist, he would often move to the front of the stage and play bass while singing, with Doughty assuming drum duties. By early 1968, guitarist Matt had graduated and departed, replaced by Bob Crownover. A fifth member, singer Terry Luttrell, joined around the same time. Luttrell started as a guitar player and had been in bands like Terry Cook and The Majestics and Fat Daddy Five since his early

7

teens. Luttrell said as early as fall of 1967, Doughty had approached him after a show at the Red Lion and asked Luttrell to sing for them, even though Doughty's band had no name yet. At the time Luttrell joined, he was still in the US Marine Corps Reserves.

Not long after, bassist Blair departed. Replacement Gregg Philbin, another university student, joined by mid-1968. Philbin was a saxophonist but switched to bass upon joining L.C. Borden's Condensed Orchestra (the name likely a play on Borden's condensed milk and its cow mascot Elsie). After L.C. Borden disbanded, Philbin joined REO. Horns were soon added, with Marty Shepard on trumpet. Shepard, who sometimes would play two trumpets at the same time, had previously been in King Edward and the Gaypoppers ('gaypopper' being slang for a weekend heroin user).

Although many websites claim Joe McCabe was a saxophone player in the band at that time, Shepard doesn't recall that. 'I'm pretty sure there was never a sax player,' said Shepard. 'Maybe there was, but I never heard of it before. Neal played a little bit of trumpet. Neal would often play with one hand on the organ and one hand on the trumpet.' Luttrell remembered a sax player briefly in the band, but figures McCabe left before Shepard joined. Both agree there was a second trumpet player during Shepard's time. 'We got the First Chair of the University of Illinois Orchestra to play in the band,' said Shepard. That trumpet player is remembered only as Steve. REO, at the time, was playing songs like 'Stormy Monday Blues.' Shepard said, 'One of our songs was Blood, Sweat and Tears' 'You've Made Me So Very Happy.' Terry (Luttrell) did a great job on that.'

When Bob Crownover left, Shepard's roommate and fellow King Edward bandmate William (Bill) Fiorio came on board for guitar duties. Fiorio had previously been in another local band, Lothar and the Hand People (not to be confused with the Denver-based Lothar and the Hand People). REO had started working up original numbers by this point. One song was 'Ethel,' written by Fiorio. Shepard recalled some of the song: 'Ethel works at a hamburger stand, and everything was really grand.'

Around this time, the band hired its first road crew member, Spider Lawler. They also had a van. One night, they all attended a show in Chicago at Kinetic Playground. 'We had all our equipment in the van,' said Shepard. 'After it was done, we went out to the van and somebody had broken in and stolen everything. My trumpet was stolen, all of Alan's drums were stolen; it was devastating. I don't how we were able to purchase new things. (Manager) Irv (Azoff) maybe helped facilitate that.' Shepard added, 'We each received $50 per gig when we were paying off the loan.'

At an outdoor show near Lake Geneva, Wisconsin, where they opened for Iron Butterfly, REO received its first standing ovation. Shepard said, 'We ended our set with a song by the Chambers Brothers called 'Time.' When we finished the song, all 5,000 people jumped to their feet and were screaming. We never had a response like that. It was amazing.' Luttrell also fondly remembers that show and the standing ovation.

In late 1968 or early 1969, Shepard departed REO. 'When I quit,' said Shepard, 'we were rehearsing at the Red Lion. It was because I had to decide between flunking out of the University of Illinois or continuing on, and my parents kind of suggested it. But they (the band) were very upset. They were not pleased. And I'm really glad. As opposed to 'Yeah, okay, don't let the door hit you in the ass, buddy'.' He added, 'I think they got another horn player and they just didn't have the correct rock and roll feel. And I could tell over time that the band was moving in a direction that, I don't see horns in this. I saw the writing on the wall.'

While in REO, Shepard did record them on a primitive two-track recorder. He said, 'We did, I think, four or five songs.' A little over a decade later, he passed the tape along to the band, but it has never surfaced.

In the meantime, the revolving roster of REO members continued. By summer 1969 the horn section was gone and the band was moving more toward rock than soul or blues. Guitarist Fiorio served a few months before moving on to pursue his passion for the blues. Fiorio became well-known as Doctor Duke Tumatoe, and after leaving REO, he formed The All-Star Frogs, and later The Power Trio.

Around this time, Doughty acquired his nickname. On the 23 May 2020 YouTube episode of Holly Cronin's *Holly Picks*, Doughty explained it was his near-infatuation with Captain Beefheart's 1969 *Trout Mask Replica* album title and cover (more so than the music itself) that earned him the moniker 'Trout,' which is still with him today.

With Shepard and Fiorio gone and Philbin on board, four-fifths of the band that appeared on the first REO record was in place: Gratzer (drums), Doughty (keyboards), Luttrell (vocals), and Philbin (bass). Fiorio's departure opened the door for guitarist Steve Scorfina, then playing in Cyro Flash Cat in the St. Louis area. Scorfina started his first band, Mike and Majestics, at age 13. One of his bandmates at the time was 11-year-old Michael McDonald, later of Steely Dan, Doobie Brothers, and solo fame.

Scorfina said Azoff, the band's manager, called him but the phone connection was bad and full of static. Scorfina said, 'I couldn't understand (Azoff). I thought he said Illinois Speed Press (featuring Paul Cotton, later of Poco). And I went, 'Illinois Speed Press. That's one of my favourite bands. Of course, I'm coming up and auditioning with them.' So I came up to Champaign to audition with the Illinois Speed Press and when I got there, I looked at the drum head and it said REO Speedwagon on it. And I went, 'Oh my God, what is this?' But I listened to them and they sounded fabulous. I've played in about maybe 40 bands in my life and when I heard those guys, I knew that they were gonna make it. From Day One.'

The guitarist echoed trumpeter Shepard's recollections on the band's schedule. 'That group was the hardest working band I've ever been in,' said Scorfina. 'Irving (along with business partner Nutt) had a booking agency called Blytham Limited. They kept us working five, six nights a week. And we'd play up in Wisconsin, played in Chicago, played down in Carbondale (Illinois), over to Indiana. We'd always come back to Champaign, and we were like the house band every two weeks at the Red Lion. Also, the Red Lion was open for us to practice at.'

Scorfina continued, 'We had two roadies and they would set up our equipment and we'd practice all day and play all night. They were a hard, hard, working band. When I joined the group, we started writing songs. The first song we worked out was 'Sweet Lucille'.' It was Scorfina who pushed the band toward the heavier, more guitar-based sound that formed the first REO album. 'We were more like the MC5 than what (REO) later became,' he said. At their shows, the closer became The Rolling Stones' 'Sympathy for the Devil,' with Scorfina on lead vocals.

'I was a conscientious objector and totally against the war,' said Scorfina, who has continued to volunteer with military veterans organizations over the years. 'When I joined the band, I specifically told them, 'I don't care what music we do, but my main thing is Stop the War in Vietnam. And I want to do as many things as I can against the war in Vietnam'.' Which is how REO's biggest gig with this line-up came about, in front of a daytime crowd of 20,000 (or up to 60,000, depending on the source) people at the Moratorium on War rally in Chicago. It was held outside Mayor Daley's office, garnering national attention for the band.

Fellow Champaign student Arnie White captured the event in a series of photographs. His photos from that day show a massive crowd and a phalanx of news cameras on scaffolding filming the event from across the plaza. After performing, the band returned to their hotel and watched themselves on national and local news shows. The Huntley-Brinkley Report opened its segment with a clip of REO performing 'Sympathy for the Devil.'

That evening, the entire band was invited to Hugh Heffner's Playboy Mansion, where they mingled with actor Dennis Hopper, activists The Chicago Seven (whom they had only hours earlier invited up on stage to sing backup on one of their songs), singer Michelle Phillips, and others. Later that night, guitarist Scorfina and photographer White ended up at a club called Beaver's, where they met Ron Wood and Rod Stewart.

At one point during Scorfina's tenure in the band, they made their way to Golden Voice Recording Company studios in Pekin, Illinois. There, they recorded at least four songs, including 'Sweet Lucille' and 'Gypsy Woman's Passion,' the latter of which appeared on the first REO Speedwagon album in 1971. Many musicians working in central Illinois in the late 1960s and early 1970s, including Gidian's (sic) Bible and Head East, made use of Golden Voice studios. Unfortunately, the facility burned down in 1977 and any recordings housed at the studio were lost forever.

From the start, creative tension has always been a strength of REO, and Scorfina and singer Luttrell were sometimes at odds regarding the direction of the band. At one point, Scorfina recalled, 'I even said to Irving (Azoff), if you want me to stay with the group, you need to hire Mike Murphy.' Of course, that didn't happen at the time. And any differences between Scorfina and Luttrell have long since been resolved, with the two performing on stage together as recently as 2019.

Eventually, Scorfina, tired of the drama and drugs in REO and advised he was leaving. Scorfina said, 'I'd actually seen Gary Richrath. He was at the Red Lion; he was in a band called Feather Train. I told him, I said, 'Listen, Gary. I'm leaving REO and I know you love the band,' cause he would come see us all the time. So he knew I was going to be gone and he was right there when I was gone.' Not long after his departure from REO, Scorfina formed progressive rock band Pavlov's Dog, who earned massive success in St. Louis and had a growing fanbase throughout the Midwest. He performed with the band from 1972-1977, and again in 2004.

Luttrell has also said he recommended Richrath because he'd seen him in Feather Train, but initially, Richrath resisted. Luttrell said to convince Richrath to join, 'I gave him my last 50 bucks' to make it to the audition.

Richrath initially learned music on the saxophone, later teaching himself guitar after receiving one from his uncle Leroy. Upon graduating from high school, he joined the band Suburban 9 to 5, playing local venues and recording a few singles at Golden Voice studios. In March 1968, Suburban 9 to 5 was an opening act at a show for The Who at the Opera House in Exposition Gardens in Peoria, Illinois. Another local act on the bill was The New Coachmen, whose members included Dan Fogelberg. Sometime later, in 1968, Richrath left Suburban 9 to 5 to join The Alliance. By 1970, he was a member of Feather Train. It was his time in Feather Train that saw the guitarist working with Bruce Hall, who would replace Philbin on bass in early 1977. Hall, of course, is still in REO 45-plus years later. Around the time the first REO Speedwagon LP was recorded and released, Hall was playing in One-Eyed Jacks with Michael Murphy, who would join REO in 1973 for a three-album tenure.

Folklore has it that after Richrath saw REO performing around Champaign, he declared, 'Someday I'm going to be in that band, whether they want me or not.' And so it was that in late 1970, Richrath's mother drove him to his successful audition for REO. With Richrath on board, the line-up that created that first record was complete and honing their craft through endless live shows around Illinois. The setlist included 'Sympathy for the Devil,' a holdover from Scorfina's time in the band, but more originals were making their way into their performances. It would be only a matter of time before they found themselves in a recording studio.

From that day in 1967, when they discovered their name on the blackboard in a classroom, REO had a crowd-pleasing formula that still holds true: no gimmicks, just talent and relentless hard work. Though the music evolved, the songs themselves were typically about perseverance and optimism, love growing or love gone wrong, or just having a good time.

Early recordings

'I'm a Man' by The High Numbers (Bo Diddley) (4:17) (circa 1965)
The first known record featuring Gratzer, 'I'm a Man' was a low-budget, self-produced, self-issued effort. The song and its flipside ('High Heel Sneakers') were recorded live, as quickly and with as few takes as possible, at a studio in Chicago.

Heavy on harmonica, it features a solid drum solo from Gratzer. The High Numbers modeled their performance after The Yardbirds 'rave up' style cover rather than the original Bo Diddley version (which was itself modeled after Muddy Waters' 'Hoochie Coochie Man').

'Baby Please Come Home' by The Inspirations (Murphy, Bruce Jensen) (2:27) (1966)
This is an early recording featuring future REO member Michael Murphy, written by Murphy and guitarist Bruce Jensen. The band consisted of Murphy on keyboards, Jensen on guitar, brothers Keith (guitar) and Ken Newell (bass), Dennis Milby on drums, and Don Dowd on bass. The song features prominent organ and bass and wouldn't be out of place on a record by The Animals in the mid-1960s. The B-side was another Murphy/Jensen number titled 'That Girl.'

'Sunshine Becomes You' by Suburban 9 to 5 (Scott Somerville, Richrath) (2:25) (1967)
'Sunshine Becomes You' is probably the first professional songwriting credit for Richrath. Suburban 9 to 5 consisted of Richrath, Scott Somerville on vocals, Rick Nelson on rhythm guitar and keyboards, Bubby Skinner on drums, and Danny Higgins on bass. 'Sunshine Becomes You' was recorded at Golden Voice studios. There's surprisingly little guitar featured, considering Richrath was one of the songwriters. The tune moves along on bass and organ, giving it a psychedelic flavor typical of the late 1960s.

This was the second of three singles the band recorded. The flipside, 'Captain Kangaroo,' was written by Somerville. *Captain Kangaroo* was an American TV show for children that ran from the mid-1950s through the early 1990s.

'Junk Yard' by 13th Precinct (Murphy, Bruce Jensen) (circa 1967)
Michael Murphy (keyboards), Bruce Jensen (guitar), Dennis Milby (drums), and Don Dowd (bass) left The Inspirations shortly after recording 'Baby Please Come Home' to form 13th Precinct. 13th Precinct were another act in the growing Blytham Ltd booking agency stable, with Azoff by now certainly familiar with Murphy's talents. 'Junk Yard' has a slightly heavier, almost psychedelic feel, with more prominent organ and guitar than The Inspirations had. Another Murphy/Jensen-penned number, 'You Gotta Be Mine,' graced the flipside and had a similar tone to 'Junk Yard.' When

drummer Milby left 13th Precinct in 1969 following an injury, Murphy also departed to join One-Eyed Jacks.

'Sky of My Mind' by One-Eyed Jacks (Richard Joswick) (2:35) (1969)

One-Eyed Jacks were another band that frequently performed at Red Lion. Like 13th Precinct, One-Eyed Jacks were under Blytham Ltd's booking agency. Around the time this single was recorded, original lead singer Budd Carr had been replaced by Michael Murphy. Carr went on to a highly successful career in the music industry, including managing acts like Kansas, Asia, and Slaughter, and worked as a music supervisor in films.

'Sky of My Mind' was written by Richard Joswick, the band's drummer. The horns on the recording are out of tune, but the song received some airplay on Chicago's WLS. Guitarist Tom Kelly joined One-Eyed Jacks shortly after 'Sky of My Mind' and would go on to sing backup vocals and co-write several songs on several REO albums. John Baruck, manager of One-Eyed Jacks, worked with Irving Azoff and later became manager of REO.

R.E.O. Speedwagon (1971)

Personnel:
Terry Luttrell: vocals
Gary Richrath: guitar
Gregg Philbin: bass
Neil (misspelled on back cover, should be Neal) Doughty: keyboards
Alan Gratzer: drums
André Borly: ondes Martenot on 'Five Men Were Killed Today'
Freedom Soul Singers: background vocals on 'Dead at Last'
Producers: Paul Leka, Billy Rose II
Connecticut Recording Studios Engineer: Billy Rose II
Columbia Recording Studios (Chicago) Engineers: Bill Thompson, Edwin
Stryszak
Record Label: Epic Records
Recorded: Connecticut Recording Studios, Inc., Bridgeport, Connecticut &
Columbia Recording Studios, Chicago, Illinois, 1970-1971
Released: October 1971
Running Time: 38:10
Highest Chart Place: US: –, UK: –

The line-up of REO that recorded their debut album had been together less than a year when Paul Leka, at the invitation of the band's manager, flew from the east coast of the US to Illinois to attend a show. Leka was a staff producer at Epic Records in New York. He liked what he heard, even though the outdoor show he came to see was cut short due to weather. Based on the band's performance and the audience reaction at that abbreviated show, Leka personally covered the cost for REO to record at his Connecticut Recording Studios in Bridgeport. Production on *R.E.O. Speedwagon* was handled by Billy Rose II and Leka himself.

In addition to his production work, Leka was a musician in his own right, performing in bands including the Citations and The Chateaus in the 1960s. Other work for him around that time included producing and co-writing such hits as The Lemon Pipers' 1967 'Green Tambourine' and Steam's 'Na Na Hey Hey Kiss Him Goodbye' in 1969. Both songs reached number 1 on the US *Billboard* Hot 100 chart. The Lemon Pipers were one of many acts on Irving Azoff and Bob Nutt's Blytham Ltd roster, which may have been the link that brought Leka to central Illinois to hear REO.

The album was recorded in two main sessions. Their first trip to Connecticut saw the band sleeping on the studio floor. It was the second that found them renting 157 Riverside Avenue, owned by a dentist. Since music was now a full-time endeavor for the band, time in the Connecticut studio meant time away from their only source of income: performing. They weren't a known commodity on the east coast, so booking gigs wasn't as easy as it was around Champaign. With funds running low, the band made some money (about $100) recording a radio jingle for Night Fighter, an acne product.

Six songs from their time at Bridgeport made it onto the debut album, with another two songs rerecorded in a Chicago studio. There was little time or money to spend on overdubs. Unlike later albums, songwriting credits were shared by all five members.

Although Leka was a staff producer at Epic, he still had to shop the finished recordings around the industry. After some time, Leka finally found a home for the album where he was already employed at Epic. It was still several months before the record was released. For Tom Werman, a new Artists and Repertoire (A&R) executive at Epic, REO were the first act he signed to the label, though he'd already seen the band on their home turf at Red Lion at the invitation of manager Azoff. Among other acts, Werman would soon sign to Epic were Ted Nugent, Cheap Trick, and Boston.

In a July 1981 interview with *Modern Drummer*, Gratzer stated that one mistake the band made while putting together their first album was that they signed away publishing rights for their music for several years, no doubt costing them a fair amount of royalties.

Photographer White, who'd captured the band's performance at the Moratorium on War rally in Chicago, took the band photos for the back cover of the album. With little creative control over the record, band members didn't see the front cover (an airbrush rendering of the front grill and radiator of a Speed Wagon) until the album was in record stores. The album's back cover listed their first road crew members, Spider Lawler and Captain Billy Landrus, under 'Special Thanks to.' In that same space was listed Dan Fogelberg. Fogelberg had been playing the same venues as REO and the musicians had become close friends.

Despite a large local following, the album failed to chart anywhere. It's a shame it didn't find a wider audience, as the singing and playing are excellent, especially for a debut album, and deserve to be heard. The music on the two sides of vinyl fall under the headings of blues, country, boogie-woogie, and hard rock, along with some prog experimentation.

REO continued to perform around the Midwest following the album's release. As part of the promotional effort, the band played a 30-minute set on *The Session*, a music program on Public Broadcasting Station WSIU in Carbondale, Illinois. The host of the show said the band had completed their second album, but that wasn't the case. 'We were working on the next album,' said Luttrell, but it wasn't complete.

After extensive promotion and performances, Luttrell would be out as lead singer due to creative differences and the band would begin a search for someone new. Not long after departing REO, Luttrell was fronting a band called Mad John Fever, soon to become Starcastle, a progressive rock band that released its first album in early 1976. In total, Luttrell released four albums with Starcastle in the 1970s and appeared on a 2007 release as well.

'Gypsy Woman's Passion' (Doughty, Gratzer, Luttrell, Philbin, Richrath) (5:17)

The album kicks off with a few measures of raunchy guitar, hitting hard and fast to announce 'Gypsy Woman's Passion.' Gratzer's drums come driving in, followed by Doughty's piano and the rest of the band at a galloping pace. Luttrell's voice carries enough of a rasp to give the song even more edge.

Although the songwriting, like every track on the album, is credited to 'REO Speedwagon,' this one was written and a version recorded at Golden Voice studios while Scorfina was in the band. Scorfina wrote the music, he said, and 'Terry wrote the verse, and I wrote the bridge – 'nobody knows where we're going to' – and (Luttrell) wrote the 'walking along in the garden, gypsy roses all around' part.'

Not quite a third of the way through the song comes some frenzied guitar and drum work. The instrumental section starts with fuzzy guitar building up to a longer guitar solo, close to two minutes, then it's piano, followed by vocals before it returns to 'nobody knows where we're going to.' The track finishes with some jangling guitar notes and slight feedback. This, the first song on the first side of the first REO album, serves as the introduction to the band, showcasing the high-energy boogie rock they'd been honing over the previous years.

'157 Riverside Avenue' (Doughty, Gratzer, Luttrell, Philbin, Richrath) (3:57)

Probably the best-known track from the album and still a regular in their live sets, it's a homage to the house where the band stayed in Westport, Connecticut, while recording the album in Bridgeport. Sings Luttrell: 'Tried Bridgeport and Westport, found a place that we thought would do, 157 Riverside Avenue.'

There's long been a rumor that the address where the band stayed was 157 Riverside *Drive* but was changed to Avenue because it flowed better in the song, though that's not the case. 'It was Riverside Avenue,' said Luttrell. The rumor may be partly because of a misprint on a Columbia Records 1971 promotional record. Part of the label's 'Playback' series, the record squeezed four songs onto a 33 1/3 rpm 7" record. Side one consisted of Blue Öyster Cult and 'Messina & Loggins' (instead of 'Loggins & Messina'), while side two was Jake Holmes paired with REO's misnamed '157 Riverside Drive.' The river mentioned in the lyrics is the Saugatuck, which flows behind the house. The original house, across from a high school, was razed in 2012.

In rock and roll tradition, the song came about because the producer told the band they needed one more number to fill out the LP, and the track was quickly put together. Songwriting was credited to the entire band, but '157 Riverside Avenue' was written primarily by Luttrell and Doughty. Honky-tonk piano starts the tune, building up tension. Gratzer takes over for several measures until he's joined again by piano. Then the whole band brings in its brand of boogie rock. After the second verse, piano and bass take the lead with some funky work, followed by a short wah-wah bit from Richrath. In the third verse, the band meets a young woman before Richrath lays down another solo, while Philbin works his way up and down the bass, driving the song forward. Soon the band says goodbye to 'Miss Lena' before ending with a guitar solo and a big, cold ending, rather than a fade. There's no real chorus here. It's more of a refrain, with the line '157 Riverside Avenue' after the first, third, and fourth verses.

As Luttrell told Elain McNamara from radio station WDLJ in a 2021 interview, REO were headed to New Orleans for two nights in early January 1972 to open for the Allman Brothers. On the drive down, the band was listening to radio personality Wolfman Jack when he debuted '157 Riverside Avenue.' The driver stopped the car on the side of the road, turned up the radio, and the band got out and danced around the car. Later, when REO performed on American program *The Midnight Special* in 1978, their second of three appearances on the show, it was none other than Wolfman Jack who introduced them. The song was released as the second single from the album but was cut down to 2:56. The B-side was 'Five Men.' It did not chart.

'Anti-Establishment Man' (Doughty, Gratzer, Luttrell, Philbin, Richrath) (5:21)
The title says it all. In the early 1970s in the US, protest songs were common, whether bands were opposing war in Vietnam ('spending all that money on a stupid war in Vietnam') or fighting the establishment ('I'm tired of your treating all my children the same').

Written primarily by Luttrell, the mid-tempo song has a strutting, southern rock style to it. Doughty's prominent honky-tonk piano makes this one probably more rollicking than most protest numbers, while Luttrell lays down some gritty, soulful vocals. The end of the song shifts into a round, each instrument taking a solo for a few measures. First come drums, then piano, guitar, and bass, as Luttrell ad-libs during the fadeout.

'Lay Me Down' (Doughty, Gratzer, Luttrell, Philbin, Richrath) (3:51)
'Lay Me Down' is a beautiful number about a brief love affair where the man is played for a fool and asks the woman to be gentle when she leaves. Luttrell sings earnestly while Doughty shifts from piano to organ. Backup vocals add to the emotion. Philbin works the bass, playing a melodic counterpart to the guitar and drums. The song features some heavy guitar, but the solo is different from the one on 1977's *Live*. 'Lay Me Down' was the third and final single from the album, shortened to 3:20, but it failed to chart. The B-side was 'Gypsy Woman's Passion.'

'Sophisticated Lady' (Doughty, Gratzer, Luttrell, Philbin, Richrath) (4:00)
A strong, straightforward rock tune opens side two of the vinyl album. This was the first single released. Unfortunately, it was whittled down to 2:48, and

some great solos were omitted. This single was the only one of three from this LP to make a small wave, 'bubbling under' the *Billboard* singles chart to reach position 122 for a single week. The flipside was 'Prison Women.'

There's impressive guitar work from Richrath, indicating what was to come. This is also a fine example of the interplay between guitar and keyboards, which would help define the band's sound on nearly every album to follow. The track is about a woman who likes to let her hair down and have a good time when her 'mama's gone,' but she doesn't understand she's not as worldly as she thinks she is. Gratzer's charging momentum carries the tune right through to the ending. This was the only recording from this album to make it onto the band's first retrospective, *A Decade of Rock and Roll 1970 to 1980*, and an excellent choice at that.

'Five Men were Killed Today' (Doughty, Gratzer, Luttrell, Philbin, Richrath) (3:00)
An acoustic number, this is presumably another anti-war song. It carries a slower, trippy mood, like something from a hippy vocal group of that era.

It begins on acoustic guitar (rare for Richrath) and an instrument known as an ondes Martenot, played by André Borly. The ondes Martenot is an electronic keyboard-style instrument invented in the 1920s that could be played by hitting specific notes or waving a hand-held metal piece over the keyboard (similar to a theremin) to produce certain sounds. Here, the ondes Martenot sounds reminiscent of a steel guitar. Vocal harmonies add to the mellow, meditative feeling.

'Prison Women' (Doughty, Gratzer, Luttrell, Philbin, Richrath) (2:36)
A change of pace after the reflective 'Five Men were Killed Today,' this piano-driven number brings the listener back to no-nonsense, good-time boogie – almost southern – rock.

It's a short, to the point number with no deep meaning other than, 'There's an object to the story, don't mess with the prison women.' It's the type of song that would've had any crowd up and dancing.

'Dead at Last' (Doughty, Gratzer, Luttrell, Philbin, Richrath) (10:08)
Here's an experimental, rather bizarre track that could be considered progressive rock and may have been influenced by Iron Butterfly. The track seems to be about passing through death's door and reflecting on the freedom of release from life. It fades in with Gratzer brushing on cymbals along with repetitive guitar, organ, and bass. One of the heavier numbers on the album, it builds with a pounding, feverish feeling.

There are two short verses leading into a scraping guitar solo, then an organ solo accented with drums and cymbals. Soon Luttrell comes in on flute, followed by more organ and guitar, and about a 45-second drum solo before the entire band returns, with Luttrell calling, 'Freedom, freedom.' Richrath enters with another solo, followed by an organ break appropriate for a funeral. The Freedom Soul Singers burst in with Luttrell, singing gospel-style, 'Freedom, freedom, freedom.' According to Luttrell, The Freedom Soul Singers were born when producer Leka called a church down the street and asked them to send over some singers for the track. After an extended jam, the song winds down and finishes with an explosion.

Related Tracks
'Sweet Lucille' (Scorfina) (1970)
Driven by Scorfina's guitar, 'Sweet Lucille' also features fine piano boogie and a bit of Hammond organ from Doughty. It's an excellent representation of where the band was at the time and would've fit well on *R.E.O. Speedwagon*. The song moves with a nice groove and tells the story of Sweet Lucille: 'When I met her, I'd do anything.'

The line-up of Scorfina, Philbin, Luttrell, Gratzer, and Doughty recorded this and a few other numbers, including 'Gypsy Woman's Passion,' at Golden Voice studios in 1969. 'Sweet Lucille' can be found on Scorfina's catmanmusic.com website.

'Be a Big Man Someday' (Doughty, Gratzer, Luttrell, Philbin, Richrath) (1971) [Unreleased]
When the band performed live on *The Session* on local station WSIU in 1971, they included this number that was not on *R.E.O. Speedwagon*. REO put on a surprisingly energetic performance considering there is no audience in the studio. *The Session* host London Branch is so reserved as to be almost catatonic. He introduces the band after the first number but calls the guitarist 'Cary' Richrath. Five songs were performed: 'Gypsy Woman's Passion,' '157 Riverside Avenue,' 'Lay Me Down,' 'Be A Big Man Some Day,' and 'Anti-Establishment Man.' 'Be a Big Man Someday' is about believing in and proving oneself: 'The last words that I said to her when I left that town, I'll be a big man someday.'

R.E.O./T.W.O. (1972)

Personnel:
Alan Gratzer: drums, Percussion
Gregg Philbin: bass
Neal Doughty: keyboards
Kevin Cronin: vocals, guitars
Gary Richrath: lead guitar
Boots Randolph: saxophone on 'Little Queenie'
Kelly Bowen, Tomi Lee Bradly: Background Vocals 'Let Me Ride'
Producers: Paul Leka, Billy Rose II
Engineer: Mike Figlio
Assistant Engineers: Ed Hudson, Hollis Platt, Bob McGraw, Freeman Ramsey
Record Label: Epic Records
Recorded: Columbia Studio, Nashville, Tennessee, 1972
Released: October 1972
Running Time: 43:20
Highest Chart Place: US: –, UK: –

Kevin Cronin was a folk singer, performing around Chicago and driving a taxi
in early 1972. He'd started something called Musicians Referral Service as a way
to find new band members because it was cheaper than placing classified ads
in the newspaper. When REO were in town, Richrath spotted Cronin's flyer at
Chicago Guitar Gallery and called without consulting the other band members.

Cronin, as most fans by now know, had one client under his referral service:
himself. Richrath and Cronin met at Cronin's apartment and discovered their
mutual admiration for Elton John's 'Holiday Inn,' each believing he was the
only one who knew the song. Cronin had just written 'Music Man,' which he
played for Richrath. Richrath was impressed that he'd found not only a singer
but a songwriter as well, and soon Cronin was in the band. Although Cronin
was steeped in folk music, it was the contrast and conflict between the
acoustic and electric guitars that forged REO's emerging sound.

Unlike the debut record, songwriting credits were not shared by the band.
Richrath penned four numbers, Cronin three, and a six-and-a-half-minute
cover of a Chuck Berry tune rounded out *R.E.O./T.W.O.* As with the first
album, this one was produced by Leka and Rose. Instead of returning to
Connecticut, the band headed to Nashville, Tennessee.

Marvin Gleicher was a photographer for Blytham Ltd, and was hired for
R.E.O./T.W.O. From that beginning, Gleicher became an art director at an
advertising agency before starting his own ad agencies. In the late 1970s, he
produced music videos for Rush ('Circumstances,' 'Trees,' 'La Villa Strangiato'),
and by the mid-1990s cofounded Manga Entertainment and was a driving
force in bringing Japanese anime to mainstream America.

Gleicher's front cover photo for *R.E.O./T.W.O.* was taken during a high
school concert in suburban Chicago. As he recalled, it was at either Maine

East High School in Park Ridge or East Leyden in Franklin Park. 'The logo
(above the band photo) was shot from a T-shirt,' said Gleicher. 'The back
cover was a fun photo shoot at Vriner's (Confectionary)' a now historic
building on Main Street in Champaign. It was the band's idea to use that
setting, he said. The band liked Vriner's and wanted to be photographed
there. Vriner's is now a restaurant and bar called Memphis on Main, but the
'Vriner's Confectionary Est 1989' sign is still visible above the Memphis on
Main name. It was that stretch of Main Street that was chosen as the
Honorary REO Speedwagon Way in 2001 (renewed in 2011 and since
retired).

R.E.O./T.W.O. was the first record Cronin ever made. Similar to REO's debut
record, it didn't chart but, over time, did slowly and consistently sell. In
August 1981, in the wake of *Hi Infidelity*, R.E.O./T.W.O. achieved gold status
(sales of 500,000 units) in the US. As with the first LP, REO's second album
attained some regional airplay. Ted Habeck, from Saint Louis, Missouri, radio
station KSHE, recalled of that era, 'REO was huge in the listeners' eye and as
an on-air talent I simply could not play enough of the band to satisfy the
audience unless I played five straight hours of REO, and even that may not
have been enough.'

Toward the end of the R.E.O./T.W.O. tour, the band was including 'Ridin' the
Storm Out' and 'Son of a Poor Man' in the setlist. Those songs, minus Cronin
on vocals, would appear on the next REO album.

'Let Me Ride' (Cronin) (5:55)

The album bursts in with cymbals, drums, and guitars, on a track penned by
the newest member of the band. Drums take over for a couple of measures
before the tune settles and Cronin declares, 'I've been on the road now for a
day and a night, I've been lonesome and hungry for miles.' Philbin's bass
pushes the verse along and soon piano comes to the front. Though the lead
singer had changed, the music continued in the same rock and boogie vein as
the first record, while starting that shift toward the acoustic/electric, folk/rock
sound that later came to define them.

This is one of the songs Cronin brought with him when he joined REO. His
writing style often means it's a while before the chorus comes in and after
three verses, Richrath lays down a short, crisp solo before another short verse
follows. The song continues to escalate before finally easing into the bluesy
chorus of 'Let me ride.' The next verse remains in that realm with some
beautiful piano working beneath it all, then comes another chorus with
backup vocals.

A guitar solo builds and the band is at full force again as Richrath continues
jamming. After shifting to the softer chorus, another big build up follows.
Doughty turns in a fantastic, frenzied organ solo while Philbin and Gratzer
continue thrashing away. Gratzer's drums and cymbals lead the band to the
big finish.

'How the Story Goes' (Richrath) (3:29)

Another rock tune, this one starts with drums and guitar at the forefront. In some ways, it's Richrath's version of Cronin's 'Music Man,' found on the other side of the album. The song is about performing music 'with a flash guitar' for a living and spending time with 'a woman I love.'

The rhythm section chugs along, Cronin's earnest vocals adding an immediacy to the tune. After several verses, Gratzer's drumming pushes the song straight into Doughty's wicked organ solo and accompanies him with cowbell. Richrath holds off until the end for his low-key solo, winding down to the fade out. Though it's just the second album from REO, as the lyric states, 'Well, the dream came true and I'm laughing at you for saying I'm a fool.'

'Little Queenie' (Chuck Berry) (6:36)

REO's 'Little Queenie' includes phenomenal saxophone work by Homer Louis 'Boots' Randolph. Randolph is perhaps best known for his 1963 hit 'Yakety Sax' (later Benny Hill's signature song) but was also a very in-demand musician in Nashville, performing on numerous recordings by Elvis Presley and Chet Atkins, among others. Photographer Gleicher traveled with the band to Nashville and watched Randolph work on 'Little Queenie.' Said Gleicher, 'He did it in one take. He listened to the song and then recorded and left. He was amazing.'

'Little Queenie' starts with gritty guitar before the rest of the band enter and build up to Randolph's first sax solo. Randolph joins Cronin at the first chorus, his playing providing all the right notes under the vocals. The sax returns for the second chorus, this time louder and more frantic. The chorus is followed by a brief, crunching guitar solo, then some extended staccato honkytonk piano, after which Richrath is back for another, longer solo.

After one last verse and another run-through of the chorus, Randolph is there with brilliant sax before turning it over to Richrath for more guitar. The whole thing is loose and bluesy, an extended jam that's fun to listen to. 'Little Queenie,' edited to 3:30, was released as a single but did not chart.

'Being Kind (Can Hurt Someone Sometimes)' (Cronin) (6:01)

After the wild 'Little Queenie,' things quiet down. 'Being Kind,' beginning with its brooding, melancholy synthesizer and softer vocals, provides a contrast to the earlier tracks and makes a perfect closer to side one of the LP. At the time, REO were sharing a rehearsal space with Head East ('Never Been Any Reason,' 'Since You Been Gone') whose keyboard player, Roger Boyd, had recently purchased a mini-Moog synthesizer. Doughty experimented with it and found a sound perfect for 'Being Kind.' With that, the REO camp taped all the synthesizer knobs in place to lock in the sound and absconded with the Moog to Nashville.

The track is another one Cronin brought with him when he joined REO. It's a contemplative piece about being open and honest about loving more than one person and making no promises to any particular lover. Cronin sings, 'What you've seen is what I mean, no more' but underneath is a feeling of regret and hurt on both sides of the affair.

There's almost a progressive rock feel here. Cronin conveys his vocals with a tone of self-doubt initially, Doughty's 'borrowed' synthesizer weaves through the verses, and then it builds into a full-fledged rock number. Synths get louder and sharper, drums harder, and vocals more savage before it fades out on a synthesizer note.

'Music Man' (Cronin) (4:35)

Side two of the album starts with another Cronin track. He was working on 'Music Man' when he met Richrath and it's the first song he presented to the band. The sentiment is straightforward and sums up Cronin's unapologetic philosophy: 'Can't you see I'll always be a music man.'

It may have started as a folk-influenced number, but once the band started working on it, it became a rocker. There's a beautiful balance of piano with the acoustic and electric guitars. Drums gallop along and Richrath delivers a sharp solo as the song fades out on guitar and piano.

'Like You Do' (Richrath) (5:52)

'Like You Do' begins with pounding piano, drum, and guitar and moves quickly to the first line of, 'Well, I've seen women who cross their legs before they sit down to the table.' Here, Richrath's lyrics tell the story of seeing the other women around him, but 'no one makes me feel like you do.'

At each chorus, cowbell kicks in, keeping the tempo steady. After the second chorus, the tempo changes, tension builds and drives into a guitar solo complete with a quick slide on the strings. Then it's Doughty's turn on organ while Gratzer never eases up on drums. Following the third chorus, the song drops to a near-classical break on acoustic guitar. Keyboards float back in, drums and vocals intensify, and Cronin gives an emotional performance, with feverish singing that leaves him slightly hoarse by the end.

Ted Habeck, from radio station KSHE, when talking about *R.E.O./T.W.O.*, said, 'The two songs that rose to the top (as far as listeners' favourites and most requested) were 'Golden Country' and 'Like You Do.' This is the first REO song Cronin learned when joining the band.

'Flash Tan Queen' (Richrath) (4:18)

Falling mostly into the southern rock category, this starts with some slightly distorted guitar before bass and drums move in and the song settles into a groove. The 'Flash Tan Queen' is someone looking for wealth more than love. Richrath's lyrics make it clear she's not going to bother with someone like him unless he's a 'diamond-studded man' with money to burn.

It's another track showcasing the great interplay between keyboard and guitars. Midway through comes an organ solo answered by electric guitar, and soon organ and guitar are weaving through each other while bass and drums carry it from below. Then it's back to the verses, the lyrics telling of being ignored and 'feelin' like a flower stuck on somebody's wall.' The song starts its fadeout, guitar and drums going strong as Cronin sings about the 'flash tan queen.'

'Golden Country' (Richrath) (6:34)

If any song typified Richrath's guitar skills and is readily identified with him, this is it. The now familiar 'whomp-whomp dahhh, whomp-whomp dahhh' announces the start of 'Golden Country.' Drums enter, building up to a crescendo, then one strike on the drumhead and it drops to a confidential tone with vocals and organ before building up again. The song structure repeats that build-up/drop, creating tension that carries through to the final, extended jam and big finish, making it a perfect number in the live sets.

This is the second song Cronin learned when joining REO. Written as a protest against the war in Vietnam, Richrath took the title 'Golden Country' from a *Newsweek* article of the same name. It harkens back to the first album's 'Anti-establishment Man' number, with its anti-war attitude and proclaiming what's wrong in the 'Golden Country,' from inequality to poverty. While live music was shut down in 2020 and 2021 during the Covid pandemic, Cronin hosted a video series called *Songs & Stories from Camp Cronin*. In Episode 3, he stated when he first heard Richrath's demo for 'Golden Country,' he thought the line was, 'with all of your money, your pork and beef fed' rather than 'with all of your money, your poor can be fed.'

'Golden Country' was edited down to a 5:40 version when it was released as the flipside of 'Little Queenie.'

Ridin' the Storm Out (1973)

Personnel:
Mike Murphy: vocals
Neal Doughty: keyboards, synthesizer
Alan Gratzer: drums
Gregg Philbin: bass
Gary Richrath: guitar
Percussion: Gene Estes, Giulle Garcia
Background Vocals: (Chicks) Carolyn Willis, Gloria Jones, Oma Drake
Producer: Bill Halverson
Engineer: Bill Halverson
Record Label: Epic Records
Released: November 1973
Running Time: 36:30
Highest Chart Place: US: 171, UK: –

The third REO album was released in late 1973, and with it came a third lead vocalist. In addition to creative differences, while working on this album in Los Angeles, Cronin was misdiagnosed with vocal cord issues and advised to stop singing. Hoping to preserve his voice, he was uneasy singing too much during the recording sessions and reluctant to inform the band. This created friction with the other musicians and after Cronin's rhythm guitar parts and vocals were recorded for the entire album, he departed the band. Anybody dropping the phonograph needle on the album and hearing a new voice wouldn't find any explanation. The sole reference was a cryptic 'Special thanks to Kevin Cronin' in the liner notes.

Michael Murphy, from One-Eyed Jacks and Silver Bullet (not the Bob Seger band), and a Blytham Ltd client, was brought in as Cronin's replacement. Murphy had the unenviable task of rerecording the vocals Cronin had already put down, singing an entire album crafted with someone else in mind. Adding to the awkwardness, Murphy and Cronin were living in the same apartment building while Murphy worked on his vocals.

The album was produced and engineered by Bill Halverson, who'd previously worked with Cream, Zephyr (Tommy Bolin), Crosby, Stills, Nash & Young, and others. Two songs here were eventually released with the original Cronin vocals: 'Son of a Poor Man' on 1980's *Decade*, and 'Ridin' the Storm Out' on *The Box Set Series* in 2014. The remainder of the Cronin tracks remain unreleased.

Marvin Gleicher, who did the photo shoot for *R.E.O./T.W.O.*, was hired again for the *Ridin' the Storm Out* album cover and publicity shots while Cronin was in the band. 'I flew to Boulder, Colorado,' Gleicher said, 'and shot pictures at live music club Tulagi's. Then we went up to Estes Park and Rocky Mountain National Park and shot for two days. I sent all the negatives to Epic Records and then never heard from them again.' That was because in the

25

meantime, other photos were taken for the album cover, and after those were complete, Cronin was out of the band and Murphy had joined. Gleicher, who wasn't paid for the travel to Colorado or the prints or negatives from the photo shoot, finally settled with Epic two years later.

Bob Jenkins was the other photographer hired for *Ridin' the Storm Out*. The band was lodging at Gypsy Rose Lee's estate in Los Angeles during recording. Lee, the basis for the musical *Gypsy*, was a burlesque entertainer and stripper, and later a television talk show host, who passed away in 1970. Jenkins' cover photograph, with Cronin sitting on the viewer's left, was shot in a room at Lee's estate.

With Cronin gone, Murphy was flown out to the house, photographed, and airbrushed into the picture. A thumbnail image of the original Cronin cover appeared side by side with the final Murphy cover in *Decade*'s liner notes. A comparison reveals it wasn't the exact same shot used for both, though both were from the same session. The arrangement of the band members differs slightly, and Murphy has been placed where Cronin had been sitting. The inner paper sleeve was blue-black, with the REO logo on one side, song lyrics on the other. It was the first time printed lyrics had been included on an REO record.

The subsequent tour included what appear to be the band's first shows in Canada, in October 1973. In April 1974, REO appeared on the US program *Don Kirshner's Rock Concert*, showing off with performances of '157 Riverside Avenue' plus 'Without Expression (Don't be the Man)' and 'Ridin' the Storm Out' from the new album. The first two numbers featured Richrath and Murphy on Les Paul guitars, with the entire band singing the backup 'don't be the man, don't be the man' vocals on the second number.

Two singles were released, though neither charted. The band's relentless touring, however, was starting to pay off. *Ridin' the Storm Out* was the first REO album to make the *Billboard* chart, reaching number 171 and remaining on the chart for two months. In the wake of the band's late 1970s albums (*Live, Tuna Fish, Nine Lives*), *Ridin' the Storm Out* was certified gold (500,000) in the US in May 1980. It eventually achieved platinum status (1,000,000) in April 1989.

'Ridin' the Storm Out' (Richrath) (4:10)

The album starts memorably with Doughty's synthesizer, climbing several octaves and dropping slightly before cymbals, drums, and guitar take over. According to Doughty in a May 2022 *Ultimate Classic Rock* interview, it was producer Halverson who suggested the opening notes. The intent was to emulate wind howling through cabin windows, but it sounds equally like a storm warning siren. Doughty has stated in more than one interview that when people traveling down the highway heard the song over their car radio with the synthesizer wailing, they often mistook it for a police siren somewhere behind them and tossed their drug stash out the window. As Head

East's Roger Boyd pointed out in a September 2013 interview with *Ultimate Classic Rock*, it's Boyd's synthesizer that Doughty played on 'Ridin' the Storm Out,' but Doughty has said he believes by that time he'd bought his own.

The song has its origins from the previous year's tour, which found the band in Boulder, Colorado, performing at Tulagi Bar (named after a Solomon Island). The bar changed hands many times over the decades and closed in 2003, but the Tulagi sign remains on the front of the building. Depending on when the tale was told and who was telling it, the story behind 'Ridin' the Storm Out' varies. In some tellings, Cronin and Richrath wanted to play a joke on their manager and pretended to get lost in the mountains, only to find themselves truly lost during a storm. Other versions have the band making their way up the mountains and discovering a storm rolling in but making their way safely down before it hit. Another story has the band in the mountains and caught there when a blizzard did hit.

Regardless, the basics are the same. REO were on tour with a stop in Boulder, in the foothills of the Rockies. During their time off, they ventured up into the mountains as a storm was brewing. They made it back for their Tulagi show and Richrath was inspired to write the tune. From the beginning, it was as much about surviving the ups and downs of life as it was about the more literal interpretation of surviving a snowstorm. While Cronin was still in the band, the song received its first public performance at a club in Milwaukee, Wisconsin, most likely Humpin' Hanna's.

With Murphy's vocals, the track was released as a single, edited down to 2:29. It received regional airplay but did not chart. 'Ridin' the Storm Out' became available in April 2009 as a downloadable track for the *Rock Band* video game. It was also heard in Season 7, Episode 11 (January 2012) of *Supernatural*.

'Whiskey Night' (Richrath) (4:42)

In 'Whiskey Night,' Richrath's lyrics tell of the morning following a night of heavy drinking, most likely after a lovers' quarrel, 'and I can't see who is the biggest fool of all, with my eyes all scarred from a whiskey night.' Murphy's voice fits with the rhythm and blues tone of the track, which also makes good use of background vocalists Carolyn Willis, Gloria Jones, and Oma Drake. The three, credited on the back cover simply as 'Chicks,' add gospel overtones to the choruses. Jones later had a son with Marc Bolan (T. Rex) and was driving the car the night Bolan was killed in an accident in September 1977. Willis was a member of Honey Cone, an R&B group who had a US number one hit with 'Want Ads' in 1971.

The song starts with funky wah-wah guitar. Bass and drums elbow their way in without overpowering the mood. Organ follows and adds to the laidback feel. Joe Walsh, post-James Gang, pre-Eagles, and who'd recently released *The Smoker You Drink, the Player You Get* with the single 'Rocky Mountain Way,' provides soulful slide guitar. Walsh was a natural choice for the record, since, at the time, he and REO were both under Azoff's management.

27

After the second chorus comes a guitar break while the wah-wah and organ gently steer the song beneath it. That leads to a synthesizer solo, which returns to one more verse from Murphy. In this instance, Richrath's cure after a night of drinking whisky is music: 'Come on, guitar, you've got to save me, and get me back feelin' like I should.' There's a line in the song about how 'the river of life for you runs right,' which may have served as a catalyst for Murphy's 'River of Life' on 1975's *This Time We Mean It.* 'Whiskey Night' was the flipside of 'Ridin' the Storm Out.'

'Oh Woman' (Richrath) (2:48)
There's a southern rock attitude to the short 'Oh Woman' as it starts with guitar and then piano, telling of the unpredictability of women. 'She's happy today, it's like a breath of new life, but tomorrow her sorrow will tear me down.' Piano serves up a boogie beat under the verses as Murphy sings about the frustration of love. Midway through, Richrath steps in with a smart, rocking solo that adds to the buoyancy.

The song may be a grievance about love, but it's a rollicking, danceable tune and in the end, the lyrics make it clear that, despite all her craziness, 'Oh, woman, I need you like I never needed anyone.'

'Find My Fortune' (Richrath) (2:53)
The fourth consecutive Richrath song is a gentle rocker where Richrath handles lead vocals. It's about a small-town misfit finding his way through life, heading to Los Angeles to feed his 'crazy dreams.'

The song, like *R.E.O./T.W.O.*'s 'Flash Tan Queen' and this LP's 'Son of a Poor Man,' is superficially autobiographical, this time about a man from humble beginnings who's going to show the world what he can do and make it in the music business. The Chicks provide background vocals, adding a softness and sincerity to the track. Richrath doesn't offer up a solo, instead turning it over to Doughty on organ during the instrumental break.

'Open Up' (Stephen Stills) (3:30)
Side one of the vinyl record closes with a cover tune. 'Open Up' was written by Stephen Stills, based on his 'Know You Got to Run,' from *Stephen Stills 2.* The two songs are almost unrecognizable as being related to each other. 'Know You Got to Run' is sparser, with a folk feeling, whereas 'Open Up' starts energetically and rocks throughout. 'Open Up' adds a chorus that wasn't in Stills' original.

'Know You Got to Run' is, itself, based on the earlier Crosby, Stills, Nash & Young song 'Everybody I Love You,' from *Déjà Vu* and penned by Stills and Neil Young. 'Everybody I Love You' has some of the same lyrics and a chorus. REO's 'Open Up' more closely resembles the first half of 'Everybody I Love You' in tempo and tone.

The song arrives on a wave of organ, bass, and drums and the tempo never lets up. Walsh is back with more slide guitar and the Chicks add soul to the chorus. Richrath turns in a short solo at the end, cramming in as much guitar as possible as the song fades out. Although Cronin was out of REO by the time *Ridin' the Storm Out* was completed, he later worked with Stills to write 'Haven't We Lost Enough' for CSN's *Live It Up*. 'Open Up' was the second single from the album. It was an excellent choice but didn't chart.

'Movin'' (Cronin) (3:17)

The first of two written by Cronin that remained on the album after his departure, this one is organ-driven. It has a light, bright attitude without feeling lightweight. Richrath's guitar chugs along and the backup singers create a good vibe. It was presumably written after the band arrived in California to begin the *Ridin' the Storm Out* sessions.

'Movin'' tells of sitting in the hills 'above Topanga canyon' in the sunshine and finally discovering why 'people got so excited about movin' to California.' A couple of years later, the entire band would relocate to southern California. When Cronin rejoined REO in 1976, he moved from Chicago to California to be where the band was, fulfilling the song's prophesy.

'Son of a Poor Man' (Richrath) (3:47)

This is another semi-autobiographical number from Richrath. He came from a working-class family and was, indeed, the son of a poor man. The lyrics tell of a boy from a 'lonely farmer's town' who loves his girlfriend enough to let her go to seek fame and fortune in the big city. He feels he won't ever be the kind of man she's looking for, but he'll be waiting back home if she needs him.

The song is a nice boogie shuffle, guitar and bass pushing along on top of Doughty's keyboards. After the second chorus, Richrath offers a solo as bass and drums continue underneath before the song returns to the first verse. 'Son of a Poor Man' and 'Ridin' the Storm Out' are the two tracks from this album that most often make it into REO's live sets.

'Start a New Life' (Richrath) (3:48)

'Go home, pretender, I think this is the end here' begins this slower, piano-based bluesy track. Richrath's lyrics tell of sending off the 'pretender' and 'debater' to start a new life. But the new life is as much for Richrath as for whomever he's disparaging. He talks of 'that's only a piece of paper,' which may be a contract of some sort.

Walsh turns in another fine slide guitar performance. The tempo picks up near the end and piano and guitar provide an optimistic feeling of the situation as the music fades out. 'Start a New Life' served as the B-side to 'Open Up.'

'It's Everywhere' (Cronin) (3:42)

The other Cronin-penned number that remained on the LP, this one is a lighter rock song about looking for love, whether it's true love or free love.

29

After the first chorus, Richrath comes in with a brief guitar solo before the song repeats the first verse. Guitar and synthesizer complement each other, giving the tune a slightly pop tone.

'Without Expression (Don't be the Man)' (Terry Reid) (3:53)

This is the second cover song on the album. The track, about experiencing life rather than hiding from it, asks, 'Have you ever ridden horses through a rainstorm, or led a lion through a busy street bazaar?' It begins with understated vocals by Murphy, building emotion as the song progresses. It features no keyboard or guitar solos, instead just moving through verses and choruses. Background vocals add a nice touch, with the Chicks adding ooohhs and aaahhs and supporting the final choruses with rounds of 'don't be the man, don't be the man.'

The track was written by English musician Terry Reid, appearing on his 1968 *Bang, Bang You're Terry Reid*. In an odd tie-in with 'Open Up,' The Hollies recorded the song (then titled 'Man with No Expression' and not released until decades later), and it also surfaced on the Crosby, Stills & Nash 1991 *CSN* box set and the 50th-anniversary edition of CSN&Y's *Déjà Vu* as 'Horses through a Rainstorm,' credited to Terry Reid and Graham Nash.

Related Tracks

'Son of a Poor Man' with Cronin vocals (Richrath)

The Cronin vocal version of 'Son of a Poor Man' initially surfaced on *A Decade of Rock and Roll 1970 to 1980* and later on *The Early Years 1971-1977* in 2018. The song is, of course, very close to the Murphy version.

'Ridin' the Storm Out' with Cronin vocals (Richrath)

This is another original Cronin vocal track from the *Ridin' the Storm Out* sessions. It first appeared on *The Box Set Series* in 2014 and then on *The Early Years 1971-1977*. As expected, it is very similar to the Murphy rendition.

Lost in a Dream (1974)

Personnel:
Mike Murphy: vocals, organ, guitar
Gary Richrath: guitar, acoustic guitar, vocals
Gregg Philbin: bass, background vocals
Neal Doughty: piano, synthesizer
Alan Gratzer: drums, background Vocals
Producer: Bill Halverson
Engineer: Mike Stone
Record Label: Epic Records
Released: October 1974
Running Time: 38:58
Highest Chart Place: US: 98, UK: –

Lost in a Dream was the fourth LP from REO and the first where they didn't change lead singers between albums. Murphy was still on board, and this time had more input. Rather than being relegated to rerecording vocals, Murphy had several songwriting credits and played organ and guitar on the record.

The album cover consisted of a photo of the band members against a burnt orange background, with a housefly inexplicably sketched in the upper left corner. The back cover had a photo of the band on stage. Like the previous record, *Lost in a Dream* had a paper inner sleeve with lyrics printed on one side and band photos (including the one used on the back cover) on the other. Included under 'Thanks a lot to' on the liner notes is 'Turkey (John) Durkin (Ace pilot and general good guy).' Durkin was the band's pilot and would be referenced again on 1976's *R·E·O* with 'Flying Turkey Trot.'

Epic Record's marketing campaign included a full-page ad in *Billboard* with the headline, 'O, R.E.O.' A photo beneath the headline showed a black vinyl record sitting atop cream filling with the edge of another vinyl record peaking from underneath, much like an oversize Oreo cookie.

Lost in a Dream was also issued in quadraphonic sound, a new technology that allowed listeners an early version of surround sound rather than two-channel stereo sound. Quad required a slightly different mix of the album and expensive home stereo equipment. Promotion included a 1974 appearance on US television program *Don Kirshner's Rock Concert*. The band's performance at Long Beach, California, on 11 November 1974 was recorded and four songs were used for *Rock Concert*: 'Down by the Dam,' 'Son of a Poor Man,' 'Lost in a Dream,' and 'Do Your Best.'

Though it failed to chart outside the US, the record continued REO's inroad on the US charts, climbing higher than *Ridin' the Storm Out*, cracking the Top 100 and hanging on the *Billboard* chart for three and a half months.

'Give Me a Ride (Roller Coaster)' (Murphy) (3:50)

With Murphy now fully part of the music-making process, the album begins with one of his numbers. Murphy and Richrath play electric guitars here, but Richrath also adds acoustic guitar. It starts solidly with Gratzer and Doughty hammering away on drums and piano and Murphy's voice coming in strong and confident as the song settles into its boogie groove and moves through the first four verses.

Richrath then lays down a low-key but solid solo before Murphy repeats the third verse. Piano drives the song until it drops into a new tempo and Murphy pleads, 'Give me a ride on your roller coaster' as the band pound away before it all ends and jumps straight into 'Throw the Chains Away.'

'Throw the Chains Away' (Richrath) (2:22)

This one comes right off 'Give Me a Ride.' The music fades in quickly, with almost-but-not-quite feedback and builds up to Murphy growling the opening lyric: 'I'll be your builder.' The song is about being under a woman's control, with her planning the wedding and coming for him 'with the chains and key.'

This track again showcases the guitar/keyboard interplay that makes so many REO songs magical. After a short verse, longer chorus, short verse, and another longer chorus, Doughty takes a romp down the piano keys. Richrath dives in with a few notes on guitar, dropping a last note and handing the song back to Doughty. Piano notes climb up before the guitar returns, this time a bit fuzzier, then it's back to dexterous work on the piano. Soon piano and guitar are both soloing without ever stepping on each other. After that workout, Murphy has the final verse: 'Bells are ringing, but my ears won't hear.' The song rocks from start to finish, showcasing some impressive playing.

'Sky Blues' (Doughty) (3:20)

Relative to Richrath and Cronin, Doughty hasn't written many REO tunes. But his 'Sky Blues' is another rollicking number, keeping the momentum of the album moving along brilliantly. 'Sky Blues' tells of meeting a 'first class lady' on an airplane on a dreary day after having trouble with his girlfriend back home. He sits down beside her and tells her of his troubled love life. Though the subject matter is 'dreary,' the playing is anything but.

Philbin and Gratzer provide nice 'oo-oo-oo' backing vocals as Doughty moves up and down the piano keys. Murphy and Richrath both add understated guitar work. The song finishes with a big windup that crossfades into 'You Can Fly.'

'You Can Fly' (Murphy) (4:12)

Sly Stone ('Family Affair,' 'Everyday People') was in the studio next to REO when they were working on 'You Can Fly' and offered to play a little piano on the song. 'A little' became a lot, and piano became piano, guitar, bass, and background vocals, which probably accounts for the dreamy funkiness of the tune.

A mellow wobbly tone starts the track before acoustic guitar enters, followed by organ and synthesizer. Soon the song hits harder with several measures of a 'whomp-whomp dahhh, whomp-whomp dahhh' reminiscent of the opening bars of 'Golden Country.'

The tempo slows and Murphy sings some of his more nebulous lyrics: 'Expanse of land that would cushion your fall, as you tumble down from the sky, marble cakes of delicious design.' Doughty's understated organ, accompanied by drums and bass, provides a gentle but defined rhythm throughout.

'Lost in a Dream' (Murphy, Hall) (6:32)

'Lost in a Dream' was written by Murphy and Bruce Hall a couple of years earlier, around 1971 or 1972, when both musicians were in One-Eyed Jacks. Hall, of course, would join REO in early 1977, less than two years after Murphy departed.

Doughty is on electric piano, rather than his usual piano, synthesizer, or organ. The song is one verse and one chorus but makes for solid boogie rock about getting through the fog of life: 'You're telling me that I could be a little insane.' Philbin and Gratzer, rather than studio singers, provide backing vocals. The first guitar solo comes in casually but fits snugly into the song after the first round of chorus and verse. Gratzer's work on the cymbals punctuates the music, and a second, extended guitar solo follows before the chorus returns. More guitar leads to an energetic jam that pushes and explores yet stays true to the song. Even with nearly two minutes of jamming, the song feels like it ends too soon.

'Down by the Dam' (Richrath) (4:35)

Doughty's descending notes on the synthesizer announce side two of the vinyl record. Crunching guitar work follows and it's clear 'Down by the Dam' is another hard rock number. It's mostly a tale about a 'criminal running from the law, hiding in the high grass,' but the music feels good even if the lyrics are somewhat murky.

Richrath plays beautiful guitar licks in the middle of the track before it's back to a chorus. The last third of the song sees the band gleefully jamming away, and similar to 'Lost in a Dream,' it ends too soon.

'Do Your Best' (Murphy) (3:22)

It begins with what sounds like a false start on guitar before drums, bass, and guitar crash in on this honky-tonk boogie number. Doughty's piano and Murphy and Richrath's twin guitars bring a southern rock attitude to 'Do Your Best.'

The song is about a woman getting back in the dating game, possibly with the same man she just ended it with. Murphy offers a warning: 'But if you're gonna try and defend this man, I said you better do your doggone best.'

Doughty never lets up on piano and when his time comes, he turns in a rocking piano solo that doesn't allow the listener to sit still.

'Wild as the Western Wind' (Richrath) (4:01)

'Wild as the Western Wind,' like the song before it, has a false start. This time there's a quick blast on the synthesizer, some chatter, a few notes on acoustic guitar, followed by more studio chatter, including, 'Alright, here we go.' Then it's another blast from the synthesizer before someone counts in, 'a-one, a-two, a-one, two' and synthesizer, drums, and guitar launch the tune.

This one primarily features Richrath on lead vocals, with Murphy helping out on the chorus, and Philbin, Gratzer, and Murphy working background vocals. It's about an outlaw running 'like a crazy colt' through Native American lands of Dakota with nowhere to go. The lyrics and music give the song a country rock attitude and somehow, the layered synthesizer solo fits in perfectly. The band builds up to a big finish, but instead, it all fizzles out and the synth, drums, and guitars melt away. The original intent was probably to fade out at the end before those last drooping notes are heard, but it was all left in the master tapes for everyone to hear, similar to the studio bits at the start of the song.

'They're on the Road' (Richrath) (3:39)

'They're on the Road,' as the title suggests, is about life on the road in a rock band. Richrath helps on backing vocals, and both he and Murphy are on guitar. It's not a ballad but a gentler rock tune.

This is another track that could be considered autobiographical, Richrath's lyrics talking about the 'hometown boy in the spotlight' and telling his 'lady' his roots 'ain't in the ground, they're on the road.' The opening notes even mimic the first notes from 'Son of a Poor Man.' There are two great guitar solos here. The first comes midway through the song, the second at the end, providing a wistful feel.

'I'm Feeling Good' (Doughty, Murphy) (3:05)

The album ends on an upbeat note with this number, written by Doughty and Murphy. Interestingly, Murphy is credited with organ and Doughty with bass. Philbin and Gratzer return on backing vocal duties. The first guitar solo follows the first round of verses. The second comes at the end of the song as it fades out. The solos aren't flashy but add to the uplifting tone of the song.

Murphy sings that there's no explanation for it after all he's been through, but he's 'feeling good.' Things haven't been going well and even after witnessing 'the end of the world,' he realizes 'I'm not the only one who doesn't get his way.' It's a theme Murphy explores again on the next album with 'You Better Realize,' about being satisfied with your circumstances and what you have.

This Time We Mean It (1975)

Personnel:
Mike Murphy: piano, lead guitar, vocals
Gary Richrath: lead guitar, background vocals
Neal Doughty: organ, piano
Gregg Philbin: bass
Alan Gratzer: drums, percussion, background vocals
Producer: Alan Blazek
Executive Producer: Bill Szymczyk
Engineer: Allan Blazek
Assistant Engineer (Miami): Alex Sadkin
Assistant Engineer (Los Angeles): Don Wood
Quadraphonic Remix Engineer: Don Young
Record Label: Epic Records
Released: July 1975
Running Time: 38:58
Highest Chart Place: US: 74, UK: –

The band's fifth album became their highest charting to date, at 74 in the US. It was the third consecutive record with the same line-up, though Murphy would be replaced by Cronin within a year.

Producer Bill Szymczyk had previously worked with The James Gang, The J. Geils Band, The Eagles, and others. Producer and engineer Alan Blazek had also worked with some of those same bands, including the J. Geils Band and The Eagles. In addition to the Eagles connection via the producers, both bands were managed by Azoff. And while REO were recording *This Time We Mean It* at Criteria Recording Studios in Miami, The Eagles were also there working on *One of These Nights*. It was natural then that REO recorded a cover of an Eagles song for *This Time We Mean It* and released it as a single.

Joe Garnett, who'd done The Doors' *Full Circle* cover, illustrated the new REO album. It depicted a woman with long hair holding a smoking pistol in one hand, giving the record a western outlaw look. The back cover features a band image taken by musician and photographer Henry Diltz. Diltz was a member of the Modern Folk Quartet and was the official photographer at the 1969 Woodstock festival. His photos have graced the covers of more than 200 albums, including *Crosby, Stills & Nash* and The Doors' *Morrison Hotel*.

This Time We Mean It's inner sleeve features songwriting and other credits on one side and a sepia-style collage on the reverse. The collage features photos of band members on and off stage, a panda bear, dogs, a cow, tropical fish, a sports car, and what appears to be band manager Azoff giving a one-finger salute. As with the previous year's *Lost in a Dream*, *This Time We Mean It* was also issued in quadraphonic sound.

The supporting tour crisscrossed the US, with a few stops in Canada, starting mid-1975. At times, the setlist included a cover of the country tune

35

'Six Days on the Road,' but no studio recording of that song has ever surfaced. By tour's end, Murphy was out as lead singer due to differences in musical direction.

Since his departure from REO, Murphy's kept a surprisingly low profile for someone as busy as he's been. He's worked with Joe Walsh (including a co-write of 'Second Hand Store' on 1978's *But Seriously Folks*), did stints with Chuck E. Weiss & The Goddamn Liars, and Seal & Crofts. More recently, he toured with Pete Anderson, producing Anderson's *Birds over Guitar Land*, and played keyboards on Steve Pierson and Blues Head's *Blue Me Away*. He's also worked with Billy Vera and the Beaters for several decades (his playing can be heard on *The King of Queens'* theme song, 'Baby All My Life I Will be Driving Home to You').

'Reelin'' (Murphy) (4:30)
This Time We Mean It begins with the jaunty 'Reelin',' a paean to wine and feeling good, even though 'they say a bottle can *ruuuuin* a lifetime.' Murphy's on piano while Doughty takes organ. The song wastes no time, launching immediately into drums, piano, organ, and bass, making sure the listener understands that this time, same as all previous records, they really mean it.

Gratzer's drums gallop along and Murphy hammers away on piano as he sings, 'from drinking wine I get to reelin'.' Richrath gives a chirpy, punchy solo that adds to the buzzed feeling of reelin' from too much wine. The track fades out with Murphy repeating lines from the chorus with backup vocals helping out. 'Reelin',' with more than a minute lopped off its running time, was released as a single. It did not chart, but it certainly deserves to be heard.

'Headed for a Fall' (Richrath) (3:06)
This is a country rock tune that warns of being a little too cocky when things are going well, warning 'think about it all, can't you see you're headed for a fall?'

Guitar riffs start the tune before the rest of the band comes in, adding twang and solidifying the country rock feel. There's nothing complicated about the song, just decent piano and guitar work driving it along. Midway through, a guitar solo picks up the energy before returning to the chorus. Smooth harmony vocals emphasize the line 'headed for a fall' and shift the tempo for a moment as piano plays subtly beneath. 'Headed for a Fall' was the B-side of 'Reelin'.'

'River of Life' (Murphy) (4:19)
'River of Life' is a bluesy, laidback Murphy number contemplating fate and life. Murphy handles lead guitar duties here, as well as background vocals.

Doughty takes the first solo, piano pushing the song forward in a nice shuffle. Soon Murphy comes back with vocal effects that convey an underwater feeling as he sings, 'whoa-oh, that river of life keeps flowing.'

Then it's back to the earlier tempo, Murphy showing off bluesy, funky guitar playing and another chorus for the finish.

'Out of Control' (Don Henley, Glenn Frey, Tom Nixon) (2:51)

The fourth track on the record was a cover of The Eagles' 'Out of Control' from their 1973 *Desperado* album. The song was written by Eagles members Don Henley and Glenn Frey with road crew member (later tour manager) Tom Nixon.

It's a country outlaw number and when REO covered the tune, they added bright horns and a harder edge. Murphy's gruff and growling vocals, along with his and Richrath's guitar work, turn it into a good-time rock number. Richrath and Gratzer add background vocals.

The song is about riding into town, looking for women and trouble, and expecting to get out of control. Richrath hits all the right notes with his solo after the second verse, maintaining the high energy of the band's performance. 'Out of Control' was released as a single but didn't chart. The single is notable for having REO's only non-album B-side ('Running Blind').

'You Better Realize' (Murphy) (3:46)

Murphy's 'You Better Realize' finds him playing piano and clavinet alongside Doughty on organ. It's about looking at everything your neighbors have and trying to keep up with them: 'you got a lot of nothing, somebody's got it all.'

The lyrics remind the listener that envy and resentment won't get you far. There's a breezy feel, rather than a lecture, aided by Murphy's falsetto 'you better realize' in the choruses. Richrath coaxes a solo from his Les Paul after the first chorus while organ and piano keep the rhythm shuffling along beneath it. It's a case of Richrath talking with his guitar, making it sound like the guitar is laughing at the situation. The song ends on organ notes, followed by studio chatter: 'I don't understand, you were recording this, weren't ya?,' 'That was, I think I might have it,' 'That's right.'

'Gambler' (Richrath) (3:35)

Sweet guitar opens 'Gambler,' a song about life on the road and being honest about maybe or maybe not being faithful to a woman back home. The lyrics make it plain there's indecision about wanting a relationship or wanting to be free to experience the joys of touring. Both have their appeal at different times.

There's fine guitar work, though no real solo, aside from a few measures at the end of the song. The sentiment is 'at times it seems this life is just a bit too hollow, but the gamblin' life is the only life I've been used to.'

'Candalera' (Richrath) (3:02)

Richrath's lyrics are sometimes inscrutable, and 'Candalera' falls into that category. It's about falling in love with 'an unmarried woman,' but then 'we fell from the darkened lady, there was no fence, charm or cloud in the sky.' It is, perhaps, about losing a love to the forces of life and nature and searching for that love forever after, calling her name into the night.

The tune is piano- and guitar-based and drives forward with thick wah-wah and muted cowbell in the midsection. Even if the meaning is unclear, the song rocks along nicely.

'Lies' (Murphy) (4:33)

Both Murphy and Richrath handle lead guitar duties here. 'Lies' begins with funky, strutting licks from a single guitar, punctuated by drums, before a second guitar joins in. The second verse is sung over a quick, repeating 'whomp-whomp-dahh' round of notes that mimics the start of 'Golden Country' as Murphy sings, 'You'd lie to get your way.'

It's not clear if Murphy was aiming his lyrics at someone in particular or just writing about anyone who lies. The lyrics are accusatory: 'What you're really trying to say, that you'd lie to get your way.' The fourth verse, as with the second verse, is sung over the 'whomp-whomp-dahh' again. Midway through comes a guitar solo that complements the opening funky licks, taking them a little further before returning to the opening phrasing. Then it's back to the belligerent lyrics: 'What do you think you're doing, stepping on somebody's ground.' There could be no message at all in the song, or it could be reflective of growing creative differences within the band, as the next album would be without Murphy.

'Dance' (Richrath) (4:08)

In some ways, this is another loosely autobiographical song from Richrath, as the lyrics state, 'We said goodbye to the dusty plains of Illinois, across the road to wherever we felt the urge we should be.' Richrath handles lead vocals. He sings about how it feels to be on the road, smiling and playing, though it doesn't all work out, as he acknowledges at the start: 'Well, we have one foot stuck in the graves we're digging.'

'Dance' goes straight into the vocals after an opening note or two on guitar, with no real instrumental introduction, as if Richrath is impatient about getting his message across. The first chorus doesn't come until almost midway through, after several verses, and he sings, 'I know that some people just wanna get up and dance.'

After that chorus, Doughty takes a turn with rapid-fire piano playing that definitely makes the listener want to get up and dance. Murphy remains in the background on organ, helping with background vocals as well. After another verse and chorus, Richrath is back for another solo, as piano and organ weave in and out, and they fade out together.

'Dream Weaver' (Richrath) (5:08)

The album closes with 'Dream Weaver,' another Richrath-penned number. Murphy's on piano, with Doughty on organ. The song begins with distorted guitar, ambling along for several measures before the drums build up and organ enters to establish a groove.

This song came out a month or two before the Gary Wright song of the same name, but the songs are not in any way similar. Richrath's dream weaver is about life's dreams and what may come, rather than dreams that come while sleeping. The dream weaver could be several things, from a drug that inspires creativity and hope ('dream weaver, I'm scheming on you again' and 'I do encounter extreme pressure the moment that I deplete your fare') to some kind of deity blessing aspirations ('dream weaver, weave us that dream today').

Doughty is a deft touch on organ, playing punchy rhythms and ethereal, dreamy solos that wash over the listener. Toward the end, Murphy comes to the front on piano, climbing up and down the keys. The song fades out too soon but leaves the listener smiling.

Related Tracks
'Running Blind' (Richrath) (3:00)

'Running Blind' was the B-side to 'Out of Control.' It has the distinction of being REO's only non-album B-side over the course of their career. Anyone who's heard 'Runnin' Blind' from 1978's *You Can Tune a Piano, but You Can't Tuna Fish* will instantly recognize the track, which is a reworking of this song. It begins with the same drum intro, but the lyrics are completely different.

Here, the song is more introspective, wondering where life is headed with 'no sense of direction in my weary mind.' It's also another nod to Richrath's small-town roots and how the music business can shatter his intentions: 'If you make a country boy sing the songs he shouldn't be singing.' It all drives him to question what he's doing as he's running blind. Piano, bass, and drums carry the verses, while synthesizer moves the chorus along. Richrath waits until the end to lay down a brief solo. 'Running Blind' would've worked on *This Time We Mean It*, though it does feel the band knew it would end up as a B-side and didn't put as much effort into it as they might've otherwise.

R·E·O (1976)

Personnel:
Kevin Cronin: guitar, vocals
Gary Richrath: guitar, vocals
Gregg Philbin: bass
Alan Gratzer: drums
Neal Doughty: piano, organ, keyboards
Producer: John Stronach
Record Label: Epic Records
Released: June 1976
Running Time: 33:27
Highest Chart Place: US: 159, UK: –

With Murphy and the rest of the band going their separate ways following *This Time We Mean It*, REO needed a new singer. Greg X. Volz was contacted by Blytham Ltd. At the time, Volz was lead singer for Gidian's Bible. Gidian's Bible were out of Normal, Illinois, played much the same circuit as REO, and had recorded at Golden Voice like many other local acts.

Volz confirmed he never recorded any material with REO and never even met the band members when he was offered the job. 'They knew I was a Christian, but the question was, would I sing the material. I told them, thank you for the opportunity, but I would have to pass,' said Volz. He went on to a successful run with Christian rock band Petra, and later released more than a dozen albums as a solo artist.

John Baruck had been part of Blytham Ltd since the start of REO's career and, sometime around 1976, he shifted from business manager to band manager. Cronin, meanwhile, was playing acoustic shows around northern Illinois and had stayed in touch with Baruck. He'd even sent Baruck a demo tape of songs he'd written during his time away from REO. When it came time to record *R·E·O*, Cronin was back in, along with his demos. One of those demos was rejected outright by producer John Stronach and the rest of the band. The song, 'Time for Me to Fly,' did make it onto the band's next studio album, 1978's *Tuna Fish*.

The band obviously had faith in the songs that did make it onto the LP, with five of eight tracks appearing on the following year's live release. The songs on *R·E·O* were great, the performances were strong, the album featured fantastic harmony vocals, but something was lost in the recording process. Drums, bass, and keyboards didn't always shine like they should've. It's not until a listener compares the studio versions to the soon-to-follow live renditions that the difference is clear.

The album cover was simple, maybe too simple for a Midwest act trying to break nationally. The original intent was to have R·E·O branded onto a horse, but the artwork ended up being R·E·O stamped on cowhide. It didn't take long for fans, and even band members, to call the record 'the COW album' or simply

C·O·W. The back cover is a beautiful monochrome band shot by Lorrie Sullivan, who later took photos for *Live*. That photo might've made a better front cover than cowhide. Here, Richrath has his arms wrapped around Doughty and Gratzer, Philbin's arm is over Cronin's shoulder, everyone looking happy. On the lower left was the song listing and producer credit. The inner sleeve was plain white paper.

The album and the 'Keep Pushin'' single officially removed 'Speedwagon' from the band's name, with both displaying just R.E.O. That wouldn't last, and by the next record, it would be back to the full R.E.O. Speedwagon moniker, before becoming REO Speedwagon (without the periods) by *Tuna Fish*.

After three successive albums reaching the *Billboard* 200, each climbing higher than the last, *R·E·O* seemed a commercial step backward. This, the band's sixth album, featured eight tracks, all of which deserved airplay, yet it made it only to 159 and slipped off the charts after five weeks.

'Keep Pushin'' (Cronin) (4:05)
The first album with Cronin back in the fold opens with one of his tunes, which he started writing not long after 'Music Man' from *R.E.O./T.W.O.* The song carries a familiar theme about perseverance and resilience, similar to 'Ridin' the Storm Out.' It was as much a message to listeners as it was to Cronin himself.

Strong acoustic guitar strumming complements electric guitar, further setting the framework for the acoustic/electric combination to follow on every REO album. Solid harmonies and background vocals add to the beauty of the track. Richrath's solo after the chorus conveys optimism and hope without being overly complicated. The solo leads into the final verse, the payoff, where 'it's comin' together' and 'every day I wake a little bit higher.' Another guitar solo follows, then synth and guitar wind it down.

The track was released as a single, with two different B-sides, but did not chart. In Ron Stevens' 2021 *Keep Live Alive Saint Louis* film, Cronin said the first song of his he ever heard on the radio was 'Keep Pushin'' on KSHE in 1976.

'Any Kind of Love' (Richrath) (3:35)
Acoustic and electric guitars kick off 'Any Kind of Love,' with Gratzer adding a muted cowbell before it builds up to the first verse. Cronin sings most verses, but Richrath assists. The lyrics tell of accepting an unrequited love and waiting without bitterness to see if things will change. The emotional tone is at odds with the lyric content, and the music is upbeat even if the subject isn't.

After several verses, the tempo slows and Richrath comes in with a country-flavored solo. The chorus follows before the tempo picks up again before ending with 'oooh-oooh' harmony vocals.

'(Only a) Summer Love' (Richrath) (4:40)
Richrath works lead vocals on his own, reminding himself that the affair in question wasn't meant to last and he shouldn't waste time thinking about

41

what might've been. Like 'Any Kind of Love,' the song has a country flair. The track eases in with guitar strumming, lightly bounding forward before a few heavy measures hit with organ, bass, and drums. Richrath begins, 'Now there's nothin' left to do but to lay my head down for sleeping.' The chorus brings harmony vocals on 'But I guess it was only a summer love.'

Doughty plays organ in more of a rhythm role, carrying the tune along. The instrumental break has Richrath casually tossing out a solo, never rushing, never crowding the song structure as he hits all the right notes without showing off. After the final chorus, we get treated to another guitar solo as the song winds down, creating a nostalgic feeling for times gone by. The song manages to be breezy without becoming lightweight, a performance that evokes a warm summer day and the memories that go with it.

'(I Believe) Our Time is Gonna Come' (Cronin) (5:05)

This begins with stabbing electric guitar and insistent piano, contrasting with the previous songs. Whereas those last two numbers had an acceptance of love that wasn't all that it could be, this one is harder-edged, both musically and emotionally. Cronin's vocals are more pleading, and any hope is mixed with desperation.

Gratzer's drumming shines, and Doughty moves between piano and synthesizer. Richrath cuts through at the right moments, then solos after the first chorus. Mid-song, it drops into a groove, Philbin playing a subtle bassline and Richrath tapping on his guitar. Synth violins come in before Doughty solos on piano. He runs through single notes the first time around, then doubles up for a second round. Richrath strikes a note and escalates into a solo with some frenzied vocals from Cronin to wrap it up.

'Breakaway' (Richrath, Cronin) (4:12)

The opening of side two of the vinyl record features Richrath and Cronin trading lead vocals and harmonizing again, and like some of the songs on side one, this carries a country influence. It's another tune about persevering and making positive changes in one's life: 'It's never too late to breakaway.'

Keyboards propel the track, with a short guitar break coming toward the end. Doughty displays great piano work, sometimes pounding away over his own synths, which are part of the rhythm section. Piano climbs and darts through the verses, then soars in the instrumental section with notes sharp and clear. After the final chorus, Gratzer works the cymbals, Philbin plays subtle bass runs while guitars and synthesizer build tension until the song is back at full speed through the fadeout.

'Flying Turkey Trot' (Richrath) (2:35)

'Flying Turkey Trot' is one of only two instrumentals on an REO record. It starts with Richrath's Gibson, conjuring up the image of a turkey strutting across a field. The song is funky, it rocks, it grooves, it's everything an instrumental should be, except it's too short. The focal point is, of course, Richrath's infectious playing. He layers guitars, playing lead and sometimes rhythm. Halfway in, Gratzer's drums push into double time for a while. Eventually, Doughty's synthesizer takes over for a brief solo and then it's back to Richrath.

By this point in their career, the band had a private aircraft, though that's not as glamorous as it seems. It started as an efficient way to get to shows that were a little too far away to drive, allowing REO to return home immediately after the performance, often arriving in time for last call at closing time at Red Lion. There was also at least one beer run featuring in the aircraft's history. The first plane was a six-seater, later a Cessna 402 ten-seater, and still later a Howard 250.

John 'Turkey' Durkin, mentioned in the liner notes for *Lost in a Dream*, was the band's pilot. 'Flying Turkey Trot' is an ode to Durkin and the airplane itself. It was the B-side to later pressings of 'Keep Pushin'.' This studio version also served as the B-side to the following year's live 'Keep Pushin'' single.

'Tonight' (Richrath) (3:20)

'Tonight' is another number featuring Richrath on lead vocals. It's an uncomplicated song about being away from home – probably out on the road with the band – with work and life getting more unbearable until at last, it's time to return home to the woman he loves. Richrath pulls beautiful tones from his guitar, offering an easy-going solo. Drums add weight to the track, the synth again providing rhythm. Before it's over, Richrath gives one more unrushed solo. 'Tonight' is a lean and light uplifting track. It was the B-side to initial pressings of 'Keep Pushin'.'

'Lightning' (Richrath, Cronin) (5:55)

A beautiful closing track, 'Lightning' is the second of two cowrites on the album. It fades in with a dark, moody, mystical feeling: 'Call the wind out, call out the thunder.' The song lends itself to great visuals of a powerful storm rolling in with change and a charge in the air. On the surface, it may be taken as simply an ode to the power of storms. It could also be taken as a song about a beautiful, untamed woman ('You're the storm inside my soul that's raging out of control') who might be had, if only for one night. Like many other REO songs, it's also about the rough ride through life.

Cronin delivers excellent, strong vocals, providing a sense of urgency and turbulence while Doughty's synthesizer moves the song along. The tempo slows a bit and Richrath drops a bluesy solo before the final verse, giving a temporary sense of calm, then returns for another solo at the end, playing faster as the storm builds during the song's fadeout.

Live – You Get What You Play For (1977)

Personnel:
Gregg Philbin: bass guitar, background vocals
Alan Gratzer: drums, background vocals
Gary Richrath: lead guitar, vocals
Neal Doughty: keyboards
Kevin Cronin: lead vocals, rhythm guitar
Recorded: Memorial Hall, Kansas City, Kansas; Convention Centre, Indianapolis,
Indiana; Keil Auditorium, St. Louis, Missouri; Electric Ballroom, Atlanta, Georgia
Producers: Gary Richrath, John Henning, John Stronach
Engineers: John Stronach, John Henning, Bruce Hensal, Jack Crymes, Kelly
Kotera, Mike Klink, Pete Carlson, Rich Sanchez
Released: January 1977
Running Time: 77:47
Highest Chart Place: US: 72, UK: –

The band members always knew their strength was in their live shows. No
matter how great the playing in the studio, it didn't always capture the wild
energy and performances they were known for. After six studio albums and
perhaps 2,000 shows, was it possible REO had peaked?

Fans had told REO they loved the concerts but found the studio albums
sometimes lacking. The band agreed. With Cronin back, they approached Epic
with the intent of making their next album a live one. It must've been a
gamble for the record label. *C·O·W* barely grazed the charts. REO hadn't yet
produced a hit single. A double album would carry a higher retail price. If
fans hadn't bought earlier albums, would they pay for a double set? Yet Epic
agreed. The success of double live albums for Kiss in 1975 and Peter
Frampton in 1976 may have paved the way.

Although the band was relegated to playing smaller venues or support slots
outside the Midwest, the performances for the live release were recorded at
headlining sets at four mid-size venues over four nights. Fourteen songs and a
guitar solo made the cut. Everything was moving forward until the band
heard the first mix. This was not the record they knew they'd performed. All
traces of the audience had been stripped away. It was a thin, sterile sound, no
better than what they'd been unhappy with on some studio recordings.

It was a watershed moment. The only way to get the sound REO wanted
was to produce themselves. Richrath took over, with Cronin in an uncredited
role. The result was *Live – You Get What You Play For*, the band's sense of
humor on display with the title. From the opening announcement of, 'Epic
Recording artists, REO Speedwagon,' to the last notes of 'Golden Country'
(with a few Star-Spangled Banner notes tossed in) and Cronin telling the
crowd, 'Y'all have a happy Halloween, now, will ya – we'll see you next time,
thank you,' *Live* was a showcase of the abilities and hunger of all five band
members. Although *Lost in a Dream* and *This Time we Mean It* were not

represented, the record still served to tidy things up from the rotating roster of lead singers and let fans know what REO were all about. It was a statement as much as it was an album of raw rock music.

This was many listeners' introduction to the extended version of '157 Riverside Avenue,' originally from the debut album. Doughty's first piano notes are instantly recognizable, building anticipation before Gratzer comes charging in on drums. Philbin plays funky runs up and down the bass throughout and performs a great solo toward the middle of the song. Cronin tells the crowd, 'Oooh, yeah. That bass sounds good to me. That's Regis on the bass guitar.' Cronin was undoubtedly making a joke, referring to Regis Philbin, who hosted a television morning talk show in Los Angeles and later gained fame on a national level in the US. Cronin then works up the audience with a tale of talking to Richrath over the phone, his scat vocals sparring with the guitar.

Side four of the original vinyl release is labeled 'Encores,' and begins with Cronin announcing what the band was about and what the audience wanted: 'Let me tell ya. The show is over, folks. Alright? The party is starting right now!'

Live is the last record with a Richrath lead vocal ('Any Kind of Love,' '(Only a) Summer Love'). Interestingly, Richrath handled most lead vocals on his 'Son of a Poor Man' earlier in the tour, but by the time of this recording, Cronin had assumed lead vocal duties for the song. *Live* is also the last record with Philbin, after nearly nine years playing bass with REO. Around the time the double album was released in early 1977, replacement Bruce Hall was on tour with REO.

Hall was playing a show with the Jesse Ross Band at Ted's Warehouse in Charleston, Illinois, when Richrath called him between sets and asked if he wanted to join REO. In reality, it was more of an order than a request, and Hall was immediately on his way to California, where he rehearsed with the band for less than a week before they headed out on tour. Hall's connection to REO went beyond working with Richrath in Feather Train. As he explained in *Vintage Guitar* in December 2009, Hall acquired his 1965 Fender Jazz bass, known affectionately as 'Butter,' back when he was 16 years old. In a twist of fate, he bought the bass from none other than Philbin, shortly before Philbin joined REO.

For Philbin, his departure came down to a combination of creative differences as the band's direction started to change and frustration that REO hadn't yet broken through nationally. Ironically, then, it was *Live* that garnered the band's first Top 100 single (at number 94) in 'Ridin' the Storm Out' and earned the band its first US gold record (sales of 250,000 for a double album in the 1970s) in August 1977. The record company even flew REO to London and presented the gold award at its annual world convention.

Live peaked at number 72 in the US, the highest chart placement for the band to that point. Years of hard work and endless touring were paying off and by the end of 1978, *Live* was platinum (500,000 for a double album).

In June 1977, the UK's Judas Priest played their first US shows in Texas supporting REO. It was at Busch Stadium in St. Louis on 9 July, long before they could pull in huge crowds in other parts of the US, that REO headlined radio station KSHE's sold-out Superjam concert. Along with Ted Nugent, support acts included Head East and Judas Priest. According to the *St. Louis Post-Dispatch*, the 45,000 ticket holders were 'the largest crowd (to date) to see a music event in St. Louis.' By August 1977, the *Live* tour setlist included 'Say You Love Me or Say Goodnight,' which would appear on the following year's *Tuna Fish*. Promotion included an appearance on American TV show *The Midnight Special* on 16 September. They performed 'Keep Pushin'' and 'Ridin' the Storm Out.' As of 2022, the album cover, in larger-than-life size, marks the entrance to the Illinois Rock and Roll Museum in Joliet, Illinois.

The Songs:
'Like You Do,' 'Lay Me Down,' 'Any Kind of Love,' 'Being Kind (Can Hurt Someone Sometimes),' 'Keep Pushin',' '(Only a) Summer Love,' 'Son of a Poor Man,' '(I Believe) Our Time is Gonna Come,' 'Flying Turkey Trot,' 'Gary's Guitar Solo,' '157 Riverside Avenue,' 'Ridin' the Storm Out,' 'Music Man,' 'Little Queenie,' 'Golden Country'

Early CD pressings dropped 'Gary's Guitar Solo' and 'Little Queenie' due to time constraints. By 2011 some versions of the CD had restored these songs.

Related Tracks
'Keep Pushin'' (Live) (Cronin) 1976 (4:05)
Taken from the shows that served as the basis for *Live*, this recording didn't surface until 2018 on *The Early Years 1971-1977*. Cronin's introduction is the same as on *Live*: 'We're doing a song now, from the new album, and it's about feeling better. It's called 'Keep Pushin' On.' It features a slightly different guitar solo, with Cronin turning it over to Richrath and his Les Paul by saying, 'Show 'em how now, Gary.' The background 'keep pushin'' vocals are more upfront, and Philbin plays some energetic bass. Noticeably absent is Neal's glissando on the piano just as Cronin belts out the 'Well, it's coming together' line.

You Can Tune a Piano, but You Can't Tuna Fish (1978)

Personnel:
Kevin Cronin: lead vocals, rhythm guitar
Gary Richrath: lead guitar
Alan Gratzer: drums
Neal Doughty: keyboards
Bruce Hall: bass guitar
Lon Price: saxophone
Tuna-Ettes (Tom Kelly, Denny Henson, Denise McCall, Angelle Trosclar, Cronin):
Background Vocals
Producers: Cronin, Richrath, with Paul Grupp
Executive Producer: John Boylan
Engineer: Paul Grupp
Additional Engineering: Gary Lubow
Record Label: Epic Records
Released 16 March 1978
Running Time: 33:31
Highest Chart Place: 29, UK: –

Often referred to as an 'acoustic album' despite the number of rock tunes on it, *You Can Tune a Piano, but You Can't Tuna Fish* came at a make-or-break point in REO's career. They'd put in a decade of hard work, touring endlessly and playing venues ranging from bars to large auditoriums, and releasing an album a year starting in 1971. The previous year's *Live* finally earned the band a Top 100 single and their first gold record. It was time to build on that and push into something beyond a regional favorite.

The band realized their best chance to maintain their momentum was to produce the next album themselves. On a gamble, they approached Epic executives with the demos for 'Roll with the Changes' and 'Time for Me to Fly' and essentially told the label if they wanted those songs, they'd have to let Cronin and Richrath produce the album. Surprisingly, the label president agreed. To get the album they wanted, however, they brought on board John Boylan, Senior VP at Epic in Los Angeles, and Paul Grupp to oversee production. In the band's quest to make certain they didn't waste this opportunity, *Tuna Fish* ended up six months behind schedule and about $200,000 over budget. A large part of the delay and cost overrun was due to ditching the first three weeks of recording and beginning anew. This was not a promising start to the making of their own records.

Background vocals on most songs are courtesy of the Tuna-Ettes, consisting of Cronin, Tom Kelly, Denny Henson, Denise McCall, and Angelle Trosclar. Kelly had been in One-Eyed Jacks, and he and Henson were members of Guild (with Michael McDonald) and later Fool's Gold, who were Dan Fogelberg's backing band. Fool's Gold also released two albums under their own name in 1976 and 1977. Kelly would show up on subsequent REO albums through 1990's *The Earth, A Small Man, His Dog and a Chicken*, providing background vocals and writing songs. *Tuna Fish* was the first to feature Bruce Hall on bass, and the first since 1973's *Ridin' the Storm Out* where Richrath didn't sing any lead vocals.

The album cover was photographed in Joshua Tree National Forest in California. An upright piano from a stage properties shop was dragged out to the desert, along with a frozen tuna and an oversize tuning fork. In the end, the piano was never pictured on the cover, nor was the desert, just the head of the tuna with the sun glinting off the tuning fork. The back cover shows a band that made a deliberate image shift, from t-shirts and jeans to a more polished, California look.

As for the album title, similar to the telling of events that shaped 'Ridin' the Storm Out,' the story has changed over the years and details vary depending on the source. The basics, however, are consistent. After a sold-out show in Champaign on the *Live* tour, the band had an all-night party at their hotel. In the wee hours, someone in the band or crew made a joke that, 'You can tune a piano, but you can't tuna fish', and the line stuck in everyone's mind even after the hangovers had cleared a day or two later. Contrary to an oft-held belief, the line didn't come from a W.C. Fields or · Marx Brothers movie.

The LP inner sleeve was blue, with a group photo, individual band member photos, and the REO logo on one side. The flip side provided album credits and song lyrics, though no lyrics are provided for 'Runnin' Blind' and 'Say You Love Me or Say Goodnight.' Curiously, neither the back cover nor the inner sleeve list the songs in the same running order as they play out on the record.

Tuna Fish successfully balanced Cronin's folk with Richrath's rock. This was the band's first album to make *Billboard*'s Top 40. Although it eventually was certified double platinum in America with sales of over two million, it wasn't the breakout success the band expected. Around the time the second single, 'Time for Me to Fly' was released, the Epic promotion team changed and REO were lost in the shuffle. As a result, the single and album suffered.

At some point during the making of the album, REO performed a show at Sound City Studios for an audience of contest winners at radio station KWST in Los Angeles. The show was also broadcast live on KWST. Epic later pulled six tracks from that performance for a promotional-only vinyl release sent to radio stations across the US.

Approximately six weeks after *Tuna Fish* was released, REO appeared in the movie *FM*, a comedy-drama about an FM radio station. In one short scene, the camera moves past Gratzer, Hall, Cronin, Richrath, and Doughty as they're signing copies of *Live* at Tower Records in Los Angeles while 'Ridin' the Storm Out' plays in the store. The band members have no real speaking roles, but *Live* is featured prominently. Although the film fared poorly at the box office, the soundtrack, which did not include any REO tunes, eventually was certified platinum in the US.

The tour kicked off in March 1978. On 11 May 1978, the Mayor of Champaign, Illinois, traveled to the band's show at the Checkerdome in St. Louis to present the band with the Key to the City of Champaign. The Key to the City tradition dates back to medieval times and in modern days, is a symbolic gesture meant to honor the recipient for reflecting well on the city. This was the first Key presented to REO but wouldn't be the last.

On 22 September 1978, REO served as hosts of *The Midnight Special*. Songs performed were 'Keep Pushin',' 'Time for Me to Fly,' 'Roll with the Changes,' and 'Say You Love Me or Say Goodnight.' The 24 November 1978 *Midnight Special* included another performance of 'Say You Love Me or Say Goodnight,' taped in Kansas City. Toward the end of the *Tuna Fish* tour, 'Drop It (An Old Disguise),' which would end up on the following year's *Nine Lives*, was in the setlist.

'Roll with the Changes' (Cronin) (5:35)

The album opens with Cronin on piano, which may give Tuna Fish its 'acoustic' reputation. But there's nothing particularly soft about this number as it combines piano, acoustic guitar, electric guitar, and organ to create what quickly became a classic. 'Roll with the Changes' is an exuberant take on meeting and overcoming life's challenges and sits well with the attitude in earlier songs 'Ridin' the Storm Out' and 'Keep Pushin'.' Doughty's organ solo is as memorable as Cronin's intro on piano.

Richrath delivers an extended, sharp-edged guitar solo, then turns it over to Doughty on organ, whose playing effortlessly complements both guitar and piano. Underlying the guitar and organ, Gratzer hits hard, making good use of the ride cymbal and Hall is playing a thick, very funky bass line that may not even be noticed on the first listen.

Cronin has stated many times in interviews or while introducing the song in concert that he started writing this on the way to meet the rest of the band after re-joining in 1976. REO had relocated to southern California and to make the reunion work, Cronin decided to move as well. He packed up a trailer and drove 2,000 miles from Chicago to Los Angeles. On that journey, around Albuquerque, New Mexico, lyrics started forming. As Cronin drove, he jotted down words on a paper bag from a meal he'd picked up at a truck stop. Eventually, Cronin pulled off the highway to finish writing the song.

This was the first single from the album, climbing to 58 on *Billboard*'s Hot 100. In May 1978, three years before the debut of Music Television (MTV), director Arnold Levine made a black-and-white promotional video for 'Roll with the Changes.' Concert footage from Kansas City, Missouri, was synchronized with the studio recording and crowd noise was added. Footage for 'Time for Me to Fly' was allegedly also filmed at the same time but has never been released. Over the years, 'Roll with the Changes' has been featured in such movies and television shows as *The Cabin in the Woods* (2011), *Jobs* (2013), *The Neighborhood* (Season 2, 2019), and *For All Mankind* (Season 2, 2021). It also became available for the *Rock Band* video game in April 2009.

'Time for Me to Fly' (Cronin) (3:41)

In the early 1970s in Chicago, Cronin wrote this on guitar and made a demo recording of it and a few others with Gary Loizzo. Loizzo, at the time, was probably best known for his work with American Breed ('Bend Me, Shape Me'), and later earned accolades engineering Styx records like *Cornerstone* and *Paradise Theater*. Cronin originally wanted 'Time for Me to Fly' on the previous year's *R·E·O*, but the producer rejected it. By the time of *Tuna Fish*, Cronin had worked out a new arrangement and completed the chorus.

The song was about his first heartbreak, knowing it was time to let go and move on. It came about after a road trip to Boulder, Colorado, with a friend. There in Boulder, at another friend's house, he discovered an acoustic guitar with open tuning, which was new to him at the time. Folk musician Richie Havens had performed at Woodstock with an open-tuned guitar, wrapping his thumb around the top of the guitar neck. Cronin mimicked that and the result became one of the most recognizable opening chords in rock music.

'Time for Me to Fly' was the second single from the album and peaked at 56 on its initial release in July 1978. The song has a country ballad feeling to it, and American country music icon Dolly Parton recorded an interesting bluegrass, up-tempo version for her 1989 *White Limozeen* album. The song was also used in an Illinois tourism promotion called 'Time for Me to Drive' in May 2021, as Covid restrictions were easing around the US and the state was vying for tourists. The television commercial featured actors singing 'Time for me to drive' instead of 'Time for me to fly.'

'Time for Me to Fly' was featured in the movie *Grown Ups* (2010) and the band famously performed it in the Netflix show *Ozark* (season 3, episode 3, 2020). After the band's *Ozark* turn, in the 'Kevin Cronin was Here' episode, four REO songs jumped back onto *Billboard* charts. 'Time for Me to Fly' hit number 34 on Digital Song Sales, a chart which didn't exist when the song was originally released in 1978, and reached 15 on Hot Rock Songs. 'Time for Me to Fly' then showed up on Canadian Digital Song Sales on 11 April 2020 at number 44. 1988's *The Hits* also made a showing at number 49 on the Top Rock Albums chart.

'Runnin' Blind' (Richrath, Debbie Mackron) (3:06)

This one originated as 'Running Blind,' the B-side of 'Out of Control' from *This Time We Mean It*, but at that time, contained a different set of lyrics. The song structure on both renditions is the same, charging in with drums and bass, but the recording on *Tuna Fish* is punchier and has a more frantic feeling.

The song was written with Richrath's girlfriend (later wife), Debbie Mackron. The lyrics are somewhat reversed from the earlier 'I was running blind' to 'you're running blind,' accusing the musician of being 'always on the road, playin' your guitar.' Richrath's guitar sound is thicker and more vibrant here and he treats the listener to a solo at the end rather than simply fading out. Cronin's vocals add desperation and a spiteful tone to the music. The song reaches a false climax, then builds again before fading out.

'Blazin' Your Own Trail Again' (Cronin) (3:30)

A ballad, 'Blazin' Your Own Trail Again,' develops from a melancholy mood but features the same encouraging sentiment as 'Keep Pushin'.' It acknowledges self-doubt and disappointment can seem overwhelming, but Cronin implores, 'It's gonna happen, just decide where you're going.'

The line about 'blazin' your own trail again' is meant figuratively but came about in a literal sense. During his time away from REO in the mid-1970s, Cronin continued writing and performing. While in Rockford, Illinois, for a show, he found time for a hike on a nearby woodland trail. Making his way through the forest, he reflected on his life and career and what his next moves might be. That was the genesis for 'Blazin' Your Own Trail Again.' A mostly acoustic ballad, the electric guitar builds over the hard acoustic strumming, coming through with a pressing tone, diving and cutting through any uncertainty to set one's own course through life.

'Sing to Me' (Richrath) (2:34)

Musically, the tone here is similar to the preceding 'Blazin' Your Own Trail Again.' Some excellent, pleading vocals mesh with heavy acoustic guitar to create a despondent feeling. Toward the end, Cronin is nearly yelling the last verse of 'I'm a-losin' spirit, woman sing to me.' Richrath contributes a heavy electric guitar solo above bass, drums, and acoustic guitar. The song ends with 'I'm fading' just as the song fades.

'Lucky for You' (Richrath, Cronin) (5:00)

Side two of the LP begins with 'Lucky for You,' the first of two co-writes by Cronin and Richrath. 'Lucky for You' is a breezy rocker, upbeat and fun with its 'lucky in love and all is right with the world' vibe. Hall lays down energetic bass lines, carrying the song from the very start to the last notes.

About halfway through, Richrath enters with blissful guitar before cranking up a fuzzy solo. Doughty soon takes over with bright, crisp piano playing. The jam continues as the guitar returns and the band plays through the fadeout.

'Do You Know Where Your Woman Is Tonight?' (Richrath) (2:51)

This one features great harmony vocals and has a country/southern rock feel. It's about being on the road in a rock and roll band and wondering if someone back home is being faithful: 'Do you know if she's sleeping alone tonight?'

Guitars kick off the tune. The music is fairly upbeat, juxtaposing the sentiment of the lyrics. The odd combination creates a comfortable, contemplative mood. The instrumental break belongs to Richrath, who coaxes a beautiful solo from his Gibson.

'The Unidentified Flying Tuna Trot' (Richrath) (2:17)
The second of the band's instrumentals, it shares its origins with 'Flying
Turkey Trot' from 1976. Another ode to pilot John Durkin and the band's
airplane, it's a too-short but sweet jam with pounding drums and bass
pushing everyone along and showcasing aggressive piano and raunchy guitar.

'Say You Love Me, or Say Goodnight' (Richrath, Cronin) (4:57)
Kicking off with, 'One, two, three, four!' the album's closing number starts
fast, sucks the listener in, and never lets up. It's a rousing rocker that featured
as the set opener on several tours, and creates a perfect bookend for the LP,
balancing 'Roll with the Changes' at the start.
   Everyone is at full tilt, unleashed, playing as if they're on fire. Richrath is a
buzz saw tearing through the song and Doughty is in constant motion, racing
up and down the keys. Lon Price contributes a blazing saxophone solo in the
jam in the second half of the song. It's the perfect bridge between Richrath's
guitar and Doughty's piano. Price would return to play more sax on *Life as
We Know It*'s 'Tired of Gettin' Nowhere.'

Related Tracks
Live Again (Live album promotional Release for US Radio Airplay)
(31:41) (1978)
Taken from a show performed on KWST (now KPWR/Power 106) for radio
station contest winners, *Live Again* was another showcase for the band's
prowess on stage in front of an audience. The resulting promotion-only album
culled from the performance showcased six songs that had made their live
debut on *You Get What You Play For*: 'Son of a Poor Man,' '(I Believe) Our
Time is Gonna Come,' 'Flying Turkey Trot,' 'Keep Pushin','' 'Ridin' the Storm
Out,' and an 11-and-a-half minute version of '157 Riverside Avenue.' The band
were obviously having a good time and the only disappointment is that
whatever else was recorded at the show has never been released. *Live Again*
was included in *The Early Years 1971-1977*.

'Blazin' Your Own Trail Again' by REO Haywagon (Cronin)
Sometime in 2002, Cronin headed to Nashville with the idea of recording
some REO songs with country singers. The concept was dubbed REO
Haywagon. Most of those demos have never surfaced, though Bekka Bramlet
is believed to have worked on a version of 'That ain't Love,' while Gary LeVox
from Rascal Flatts sings on 'Blazin' Your Trail Again.' This country rendition of
'Blazin' Your Own Trail Again' features slide guitar, some piano and basic
drumming, but the only REO member involved is Cronin.

'Roll with the Changes' (Cronin) (5:47) (2009)
In late 2009, more than two years after the CD on which it was based hit the
marketplace, REO released *Find Your Own Way Home – The Game*, geared

toward casual players. Over a dozen REO songs are found in the video game, and players serve as entertainment reporters who must find a missing Cronin on the day the new CD is to be released. Prizes in the game included a digital download of an exclusive rerecorded 'Roll with the Changes' featuring the Amato/Hitt line-up. Here, Doughty's keyboards are as energetic as ever, Amato's guitar comes careening in at all the right places, and Hitt's drums are a little more forward. The mix is slightly punchier without being slick, providing an update to the original track without losing the original feeling.

Nine Lives (1979)

Personnel:
Kevin Cronin: lead vocals, rhythm guitar
Gary Richrath: lead guitar
Neal Doughty: keyboards
Alan Gratzer: drums
Bruce Hall: Bass, vocals
Bill Champlin, Tom Kelly: backing vocals
Producers: Kevin Cronin, Gary Richrath, with Kevin Beamish
Associate Producer: Alan Gratzer
Production Assistance: Gary Lubow
Engineers: Kevin Beamish, Gary Lubow
Assistant Engineers: Steve Williams, D.C. Snyder
Record Label: Epic Records
Released: 20 July 1979
Running Time: 34:14
Highest Chart Place: US: 33, UK: –

By the late '90s, Epic certainly wasn't losing money on REO, but the company wasn't making a lot, either. It was a precarious balance that meant the band were perpetually close to being dropped by the label. They had to prove themselves each time out, making a record true to themselves while commercially viable.

With *Tuna Fish* doing well (and eventually selling over two million copies in the US) but not the immediate smash hoped for, the band's reaction was to return to a decidedly harder edge. *Nine Lives* harkened back to the feeling of their live album and proved reminiscent of their earlier sound. As might be inferred from the title, this was the band's ninth release overall (eighth studio album). It contained nine songs and is a collective statement about the band's perseverance through good times and bad to land on their feet time and again. Not only did the music lean heavier, so did the band's image. The gatefold album cover found the musicians in a back alley set, clad in leather, satin, and gangster suit and tie. Several women in feline attire surround the band members. A live black panther completed the picture.

Cronin and Richrath handled production duties, this time adding Gratzer. It was Gratzer's first official production credit, something he would continue to do for every album through 1987's *Life as We Know It*, his last with the band. Originally, the band had hoped to bring in David DeVore to serve on production as well, but he'd already committed to another project. DeVore later did successfully team with REO on *Wheels are Turnin'* and *Life as We Know It*. In the meantime, DeVore recommended Kevin Beamish.

Beamish proved a wise move. Over the years, his credits as engineer, producer, songwriter, and musician have propelled over 100 million record sales for acts as diverse as Saxon, Jefferson Starship, and Reba McEntire.

Among other hits, Beamish co-wrote and produced Angry Anderson's 'Suddenly,' later used in the Australian TV show *Neighbours* in 1987. Without a doubt, band members were happy with Beamish's work. Following *Nine Lives*, Beamish continued to partner with REO through *Good Trouble*.

At times, Cronin has said that after *Tuna Fish* seemed to have stalled, he lost some enthusiasm when it came to writing for *Nine Lives*. Yet in the album-tour-album-tour music business treadmill of the day, the studio and tour were already booked and there would be no time to sit back and wait for the muse to strike. In any case, if Cronin was having songwriting troubles, it didn't show. He still wrote or co-wrote four songs, with none sounding uninspired or second-rate.

All nine songs on this album seemed radio-friendly, but the two singles that were released failed to chart. *Nine Lives* achieved gold certification in the US in December 1979. Despite growing success in the US and a slight foothold in Canada (this was REO's second album to make the charts there), REO still had not gained entry to the charts in the UK.

Near the end of the sessions, on 7 April 1979, REO played the CaliFFornia World Music Festival in Los Angeles, continuing their push to build a fanbase beyond the Midwest. On 10 June, they played The Day of Rock & Roll in New Orleans, Louisiana, before officially launching the *Nine Lives* tour in July. At the September outdoor show at Royals Stadium in Kansas City, Missouri, the band performed their 'tornado concert,' playing through severe storms, initially unaware of tornadoes touching down nearby. More than half the songs from the new album found their way into the tour setlist: 'Heavy on Your Love,' 'Drop It (An Old Disguise),' 'Only the Strong Survive,' 'Easy Money,' 'Back on the Road Again,' and 'Rock and Roll Music.' In late 1979, REO embarked on their first European tour, with dates in Germany, Belgium, the Netherlands, and the UK.

'Heavy on Your Love' (Cronin, Richrath) (3:34)
The album launches with a vicious guitar riff, instantly announcing a heavier offering than *Tuna Fish*. The riff is followed by crashing drums and heavy Hammond organ. Cronin's vocals have a grittier edge as well, plowing through the verses on this urgent number and leaving the last two minutes for some wicked guitar and piano. There's plenty of grunting and yelping, providing a rough, primal, sexual 'heavy on your love' feel, shifting into a slow groove a bit before intensifying to pounding drums and guitars. Richrath turns in some fine wah-wah soloing here.

This is the only co-write on the album. Normally the band would work out most of their songs before showing up at the recording studio, but Cronin, as mentioned, claims to have hit a dry spell. It was only near the end of the sessions that he forged 'Heavy on Your Love.' With Richrath completing the guitar parts, the song came together quickly and earned the 'album opener' spot.

'Drop It (An Old Disguise)' (Cronin) (3:12)

Similar to 'Heavy on Your Love,' the second track comes bursting in. Drums, cymbals, guitars, and crisp piano create a raw, tough sound. The chorus continues with urgent, galloping drums and guitars, and the wild, rapid piano solo adds to the raucous vibe. Cronin defiantly shouts over the top of everything, 'You ain't got nine lives!'

'Drop It' had already found a place in the setlist by the end of the *Tuna Fish* tour.

'Only the Strong Survive' (Richrath) (3:51)

This is the third consecutive rocker, in case anyone had doubts about the band's direction on this record. Reportedly Richrath's favorite tune on the album, 'Only the Strong Survive' was also the title track to his sole post-REO work released during his lifetime. It serves as another reminder of the guitarist's talents and of the band's tireless drive and perseverance no matter how tough the going gets.

The guitar solo begins with whining notes before bending into crunching guitar while the piano works alongside. The song's fadeout is met with another guitar solo. 'Only the Strong Survive' was released as a single but did not chart.

'Easy Money' (Richrath) (3:59)

'Easy Money' brings a change of pace with its flamenco flavor yet drives hard enough to fit in with the tone of the record. On the heels of three rockers, this one eases in, with its percussion, acoustic guitar strumming, and rainforest sounds evoking a tropical feeling. And that tropical feeling is Peru.

The band's sense of humor shines through in this fictional tale of getting busted while smuggling cocaine in a guitar case across the Peru border: 'I was thrown in a cell with a killer, a convict who coughed through the night, while I laid awake with the chills and shakes, hoping for a file in a cake.' Richrath lays down a solo that starts with a sweet tone before blasting away with a harder edge. Cronin returns after the instrumental break, his vocals fiercer and more demanding. Steve Forman lends a hand with percussion. In addition to recording with REO, Forman's credits include work with everyone from Glen Frey to Warren Zevon. He continued to work with REO through *The Earth, a Small Man, His Dog and Chicken*. 'Easy Money' was released as a single with 'I Need You Tonight' as the B-side. It did not chart.

'Rock & Roll Music' (Chuck Berry) (2:54)

With Cronin's self-professed songwriter's block, the band initially didn't have enough original material and made the decision to include a cover tune on the album. This may have been a solution for getting enough songs to complete the record, but it's certainly not treated as filler. The order of the verses is rearranged from Chuck Berry's original, but this high-octane version is perfect for *Nine Lives*, with its interplay between piano and raunchy guitar.

Gratzer's drums propel the song without ever overpowering it. Doughty takes to heart the line, 'Keep a-rockin' on the pi-an-o.' He shines with untamed honky-tonk playing on this, the second Berry tune the band recorded (after *R.E.O./T.W.O.*'s 'Little Queenie'). The piano tears up the tune making it hard for any listener to sit still. Doughty is credited with tack piano. A tack piano, sometimes referred to as a junk or jangle piano, is simply a piano that's been modified with something hard like a metal tack on the felt-covered hammers where they hit the strings, providing a sharper sound.

'Take Me' (Cronin) (3:29)
The first song on side two of the vinyl release, 'Take Me,' shifts back toward harder rock after the '50s-style rebellious 'Rock and Roll Music.' Hard-hitting electric and acoustic guitars work together, giving it the REO stamp.

Forman is back on percussion. Doughty turns in some nice Moog synthesizer work, and Kelly returns on background vocals. Kelly had previously helped out on *Tuna Fish* and is joined here by Cronin and a pre-Chicago Bill Champlin. Similar to 'Easy Money,' Cronin's voice grows more and more fierce, raging over the 'oooh, oooh' background vocals toward the end.

'I Need You Tonight' (Cronin) (3:34)
A slight shift from 'Take Me,' 'I Need You Tonight' may initially feel lightweight, but that's deceptive. This is a straightforward love song, with lines like, 'Something happens when I hold you, that makes everything alright,' though it's not really a power ballad. It does serve as a hint of what's to come on later records.

The twangy electric and acoustic guitar work give the song a country flair. The piano accompanying the verses moves the song along in buoyant fashion. Cronin's vocals are intentionally softer and less raw than on the rest of the album. Bass lines weave melodically in and out of the verses, through the choruses, and nicely support the piano solo. The piano break is nothing short of phenomenal. Sharp playing and crisp notes cascade through the mid-section of the song, begging the listener to hit repeat to hear the solo again. 'I Need You Tonight' would've been equally at home on either *Tuna Fish* or *Hi Infidelity*.

'Meet Me on the Mountain' (Richrath) (4:04)
Drums and guitar burst in to announce a return to a harder sound after 'I Need You Tonight.' Organ swirls, building up to the first verse, which sets the scene: 'I remember well, that day last spring, when the snow lay deep on the mountain trails.'

Richrath's lyrics paint a visual of two lovers meeting in the snowy mountains for a final fling before going their separate ways. There's no regret, just a sweet reminiscence of their last time together and perhaps a hope for one more. The guitar solo creeps in after the second chorus, first drawing out a few notes, then escalating before diving and driving along. After two more choruses, the song closes with another guitar solo. There's a beautiful, warm tone, adding to the 'love lost but not forgotten' feel. As the track winds down, synthesizer cross-fades into 'Back on the Road Again.'

'Back on the Road Again' (Hall) (5:37)

Doughty's synthesizer segues into this tune from the previous one, building tension, with Hall's bass soon taking over with a heavy beat, joined first by big-sounding drums, then organ and raw guitar. Hall's vocals provide the right amount of roughness and urgency. 'Back on the Road Again' ensured a strong finish to a strong album.

Although he'd been in REO less than two years, Hall was already a veteran of the road, playing in various bands on the same Midwest circuit as REO throughout the early 1970s. Hall had written the tune seven or eight years earlier while in One-Eyed Jacks, around the same time he wrote 'Lost in a Dream' with Murphy. The early version was reportedly more bluesy and after performing it with One-Eyed Jacks, he retired it for a while. It was Richrath who remembered the song and asked for it. Had there been more time during the making of *Tuna Fish*, the song may have appeared on there instead of *Nine Lives*. On any album, it would've been a good fit for REO, who were always touring from town to town, with the line 'maybe I'll see you next time that I'm around' summing up their lifestyle in a single line.

Halfway through, Doughty turns in a short gem of an organ solo, then Richrath's guitar slices through for an intense workout before Hall returns for the next verse. As Hall repeats, 'I'm on my way,' the song chugs along with the drumbeat, creating an invitation for the audience to join and clap along. The blazing guitar at the end feels as if Richrath is trying to cram in as much soloing as possible before the track fades. This was Hall's first lead vocal on an REO record and the tune immediately became a fan favorite. More than 40 years later, it's still in the setlist and deservedly so.

Related Recordings

'Only the Strong Survive' by Richrath Band (Richrath) (4:11) (1992)

Toward the end of the '80s, Richrath began working with Hall, Doughty, Graham Lear, and Tom Deluca on demos intended for the next REO record. Michael Jahnz, from the band Vancouver, contributed background vocals. When Richrath and REO went their separate ways in early 1990, Richrath eventually formed a new band with Jahnz on lead vocals and rhythm guitar, and the result was the Richrath Band's *Only the Strong Survive* CD.

Jahnz's vocals on 'Only the Strong Survive' are similar enough to Cronin's to appease any fans who wanted another REO record, while maintaining enough of Jahnz's own identity to avoid sounding like an imitation. The guitar solos are slightly different, but the arrangement and aggressive performance follow the original REO version. Overall the tone is a little grittier and attitude slightly more defiant than the original, but the sentiment of 'Only the Strong Survive' is no different from when it originally appeared on *Nine Lives*.

A Decade of Rock and Roll 1970 to 1980 (1980)

Personnel:
Neal Doughty: keyboards
Alan Gratzer: drums
Gregg Philbin: bass
Gary Richrath: lead guitar
Terry Luttrell: vocals
Kevin Cronin: vocals, acoustic guitar, piano
Michael Murphy: vocals, guitar, keyboards
Bruce Hall: bass
Record Label: Epic Records
Released: April 1980
Running Time: 96:32
Highest Chart Place: US: 55, UK: –

A gatefold two-LP retrospective, this 19-song collection allowed old fans to look back at the first ten years of the band's history and gave newer fans a solid introduction to all things REO. It also allowed the members a slight break from the recording/touring cycle and provided the time necessary to create what would become their most commercially successful release, *Hi Infidelity*.

With fans accustomed to an album a year from REO, *Decade* was released nine months after *Nine Lives*. It served to satisfy the marketplace, keep REO visible, and ensure the momentum that had been building since 1967 wouldn't dissipate. *Decade* came with an excellent souvenir booklet telling the band's story and contained at least one song from every LP to that point. For some, it provided their first taste of the debut album, which had often proved difficult to find after 1971.

The album contained several treats. Beamish, who had served as a producer on *Nine Lives*, remixed many of the older songs, from 'Son of a Poor Man' through 'Lightning,' making them brighter without losing anything from the originals in the process. 'Son of a Poor Man' – the one famously recorded with Cronin then overdubbed with Murphy on vocals – officially gives listeners for the first time the Cronin vocal version. It also includes the original six or seven seconds of guitar intro that didn't make it onto the 1973 release. Unfortunately, 'Lost in a Dream' is whittled down from 6:32 to 3:45, dropping the extended jam and Richrath's fantastic guitar work at the end.

Side three consists of live recordings. Two ('Like You Do,' 'Flying Turkey Trot') are from 1977's *Live*, and two are new recordings featuring Hall on bass. '157 Riverside Avenue' stretches out to over 12 minutes, with Gratzer getting a serious workout the entire time. During the anticipated and extended vocal/guitar exchange, Cronin shouts that well-known line, 'There ain't nobody who talks with their guitar the way Gary does.' A new 'Ridin' the Storm Out' follows. Cronin provides the introduction as Doughty's synthesizer swirls: 'My friends, I got time for one last story for ya before we have to leave tonight. You see, if ya ever been in the Rocky Mountains after the wind comes up and the sun goes down, you can find yourself in a whole lot of trouble, people. But what you gotta do is keep yourself together, keep everybody warm, and always remember, to keep ridin' the storm out, people. Come on with us one more time!'

Side four is dedicated to *Tuna Fish* and *Nine Lives*, closing out with the latter's 'Back on the Road Again.' The song was fitting for a band that was spending hundreds of days on tour every year and would be on the road once more in support of this compilation.

The only real complaint about *Decade* is there are too few songs from the Luttrell and Murphy records, and no recordings featuring Richrath on lead vocals. The album clocks in generously at more than 90 minutes, but had there been no time constraints on vinyl records, 'Gypsy Woman's Passion,' 'Find My Fortune,' 'Down by the Dam,' and 'Out of Control' would have been worthy inclusions.

A rerelease of the 'Time for Me to Fly' single, with 'Lightning' as the flipside, was issued in conjunction with *Decade*. This time, 'Time for Me to Fly' was full-length rather than the abridged single from *Tuna Fish*. The rerelease peaked at 77 on the *Billboard* Hot 100 chart, but its second showing helped solidify its place in fans' hearts. The double album might've been a risk, given its higher retail price, but fans pushed *Decade* to 55 on the American charts, the group's third-highest showing to date, after *Tuna Fish* and *Nine Lives*. *Decade* was certified gold in the US in early February 1981, on the same day the next release, *Hi Infidelity*, was certified both gold and platinum.

For a short while on the *Decade* tour, 'Sophisticated Lady' served as the opening number before 'Say You Love Me or Say Goodnight' took over that slot. An appearance on *The Midnight Special* in March 1980, just before the release of *Decade*, had REO performing 'Time for Me to Fly.' By the summer of 1980, several new songs were appearing in the *Decade* tour setlist: 'Tough Guys,' 'Don't Let Him Go,' 'Take It on the Run,' and 'Keep on Loving You,' all of which would appear on *Hi Infidelity* at the end of the year.

The Songs:
'Sophisticated Lady,' 'Music Man,' 'Golden Country,' 'Son of a Poor Man' (Original Cronin Vocal), 'Lost in a Dream,' 'Reelin',' 'Keep Pushin',' '(I Believe) Our Time is Gonna Come,' 'Breakaway,' 'Lightning,' 'Like You Do' (Live), 'Flying Turkey Trot' (Live), '157 Riverside Avenue' (Live), 'Ridin' the Storm Out' (Live), 'Roll with the Changes,' 'Time for Me to Fly,' 'Say You Love Me or Say Goodnight,' 'Only the Strong Survive,' 'Back on the Road Again'

Related Tracks
'Say You Love Me or Say Goodnight' (Live) (Richrath, Cronin) (4:47)
On *Decade*'s tour, REO stopped at Alpine Valley outdoor theatre in East Troy, Wisconsin, about 35 miles southwest of Milwaukee. The 27 July 1980 show

was broadcast live on radio station WLS out of Chicago and other US stations. Opening number 'Say You Love Me or Say Goodnight' was a take-no-prisoners performance with scorching guitar and piano solos, the whole band turning in a brilliant performance and the audience returning the energy. After the broadcast, the full show was never officially released, but 'Say You Love Me or Say Goodnight' did become part of the *Live 1980-1990* CD from *The Classic Years 1978-1990*.

Hi Infidelity (1980)

Personnel:
Alan Gratzer: drums
Bruce Hall: bass guitar
Kevin Cronin: lead vocals, rhythm guitar, piano
Gary Richrath: lead guitar
Neal Doughty: synthesizer, Hammond organ
Tom Kelly, Richard Page: background vocals
Steve Forman: percussion
Producers: Cronin, Richrath, Kevin Beamish
Co-producer: Gratzer
Assistant Engineers: Tom Cummings, Jeff Eccles
Released: 21 November 1980
Running Time: 34:25
Highest Chart Place: US: 1, UK: 6

When it came time for the next record, the band found itself again on the verge of being dropped by Epic despite reliable (though not stellar) record sales and growing concert crowds. Adding to the pressure from the label, most band members were struggling with personal relationship issues in the wake of endless recording and touring. In response, the musicians turned inward, pulling together as they created what would become their biggest record. Once most of the music was written, the plan was to find a small, cheap studio to work out the songs before setting up in a more expensive studio to record and mix the tracks.

It was Doughty who'd heard about Crystal Studios, which met the criteria of small and cheap. It was also a dive that smelled of vomit and other odors, but the band set up and over the course of about three days recorded demos for *Hi Infidelity*. *Hi Infidelity* is not a concept album, yet the songs came together to create a theme, a continuity, that flows through the music. The title is a pun on high-fidelity, or hi-fi, a system used for playing music in a most faithful reproduction of when it was first recorded. *Hi Infidelity* was a perfect title for a collection of songs about love, sex, innuendo, lies, and infidelity, with the 'hi' and 'fi' highlighted.

The cover depicts a woman in lingerie in the foreground while a man in the background is playing a record on a hi-fi. The original inner sleeve had a photo of the band on one side and album credits and lyrics on the reverse. Most of the songs were shorter than fans had come to expect, the keyboard and guitar solos more succinct, and ballads came to the fore. Still, it was in every way unmistakably REO, with the band finding the right balance between electric and acoustic. Tom Kelly returned for background vocals, as well as two co-writing credits. Richard Page (Pages, Mr. Mister) also provided background vocals as part of the 'He-Man Broken Hearts Club Choir.' Page would return for *Good Trouble* and *Wheels are Turnin*.'

63

In November, several weeks before *Hi Infidelity* came out, 'Keep on Loving You' was released as the first single. Then, after more than ten years of hard work, everything changed for the band. *Hi Infidelity* reached number one in the US and remained on the charts for nearly two years. In the UK, it became REO's first charting album, climbing to 6. It hit number 1 in Canada and went Top 10 in at least five other countries, with most being REO's first-ever entry on those charts.

As part of the promotion, the band were highly visible on US TV. On 5 December 1980, REO made their fourth appearance on *The Midnight Special*, serving as host for the second time. They performed 'Time for Me to Fly,' new songs 'Keep on Loving You,' 'Don't Let Him Go,' and 'In Your Letter,' and finally 'Roll with the Changes.' In early January, the band appeared on *The Merv Griffin Show*. Unlike most of their appearances on US television, this was not a live performance, but rather lip-synced. On 23 January 1981, REO appeared on the short-lived US television show *Fridays*. They performed 'Don't Let Him Go' and 'Keep on Loving You.'

Sometime in early 1981, Cronin was offered a job as a video jockey, or VJ, on a US cable TV network that was still in the making – MTV. Cronin turned down the offer, which would have interfered with the band's recording and touring schedules. When MTV made its US debut on 1 August 1981, REO had no fewer than 11 videos and 15 airings total in the channel's first 24 hours. The band's first song to be broadcast was 'Take It on the Run,' cut short due to technical difficulties, followed immediately by Styx's 'Rocking the Paradise.' REO were also the first live concert on MTV on 8 August 1981, with a show broadcast from Denver, Colorado. The setlist included 'Don't Let Him Go,' 'Tough Guys,' 'Keep on Loving You,' and 'Shakin' It Loose' from *Hi Infidelity*. The concert was later released on laserdisc.

One of the MTV concert's sponsors allegedly requested that the 'she thinks they're full of shit' line from 'Tough Guys' be changed to 'she thinks they're full of *it*.' Cronin declined and sang the line as normal. The show was broadcast live in the Eastern and Central Time Zones in the US, and the 'full of shit' line made it through, which would've raised a few eyebrows back in 1981. The broadcast was delayed in the Mountain and Western Time Zones, giving censors enough time to make the singer's vocals drop out for a split second on that particular word.

On 21 February 1981, three months after its release, *Hi Infidelity* climbed to number 1 on the US charts. In total, it spent 15 non-consecutive weeks at number 1, first knocked off the top slot in early April after six weeks by Styx's *Paradise Theater*. Styx held the spot for two weeks, ceded it back to REO for three, and put *Paradise Theater* back on top for another week before REO reclaimed the throne for a final six weeks.

When the REO tour made a stop in Chicago, the band invited early member and trumpeter Marty Shepard to the show. Back in 1968 or thereabouts, Shepard had recorded the band on his AMPEX two-track reel-to-reel and he

Right: The Red Lion Inn, Champaign, Illinois, where REO rehearsed and performed hundreds of shows in the late 1960s and early 1970s. (*Author*)

Left: With horns, 1968. L-R: Neal Doughty, Steve (last name unknown), Marty Shepard, Terry Luttrell, Gregg Philbin. Luttrell is wearing Shepard's shirt. (*Marty Shepard*)

Right: Performing in 1968. L-R: Neal Doughty, Bill Fiorio, Greg Philbin. Fiorio soon left to pursue his passion for the blues. (*Marty Shepard*)

R.E.O. SPEEDWAGON

SPEED WAGON

Left: The 1971 debut album with lead singer Terry Luttrell. The cover artwork represents the vehicle the band was named after. (*Epic*)

R.E.O./T.W.O.

Right: The band's second album was released in 1972 and featured new lead singer Kevin Cronin. It did not chart. (*Epic*)

RIDIN' THE STORM OUT

R.E.O. SPEEDWAGON

Left: *Ridin' the Storm Out* (1973), REO's third album, brought with it a third lead singer in Michael Murphy. (*Epic*)

Right: REO Motor Car Company logo on a Speed Wagon radiator. The band adopted the motor company's vehicle name and logo. (*Steven Mertes*)

Below: The 1970 Chicago rally protesting the war in Vietnam. L-R: Steve Scorfina, Terry Luttrell, Alan Gratzer, Neal Doughty, Gregg Philbin. (*©Photography by Arnie White www.arniewhite.com*)

Below: Early publicity photo, 1971. L-R: Neal Doughty, Gary Richrath, Terry Luttrell, Gregg Philbin, Alan Gratzer. (*©Photography by Arnie White www.arniewhite.com*)

Left: Finally, the same lead singer for two consecutive albums. 1974's *Lost in a Dream* reached 98 on the US charts. (*Epic*)

Right: The third and final album with Michael Murphy, 1975's *This Time We Mean It*, was REO's highest charting to date. (*Epic*)

Left: Kevin Cronin returned and replaced Michael Murphy for *R·E·O* (sometimes known as *C·O·W* because of the cover artwork) in 1976. (*Epic*)

Right: Lyrics for Gary Richrath's 'Like You Do' from *R.E.O./T.W.O.* (*Illinois Rock and Roll Museum*)

Below: Back of the page for Richrath's 'Like You Do' lyrics. (*Illinois Rock and Roll Museum*)

REO during the Murphy years in 1974. L-R: Gregg Philbin, Michael Murphy, Alan Gratzer, Gary Richrath. (*Richard Galbraith*)

Left: REO's breakthrough, 1977's *Live*, was REO's first gold record. It was also bassist Gregg Philbin's final album with the band. (*Epic*)

Right: Bruce Hall joined REO in time for 1978's *Tuna Fish*. It was eventually certified double platinum in the US. (*Epic*)

REO SPEEDWAGON

Tune a piano, but you can't Tuna fish.

Left: REO released its ninth album, *Nine Lives*, in 1979. It marked a return to a harder sound after *Tuna Fish*. (*Epic*)

Right: Gary Richrath at Soldier Field in Chicago, circa 1974. (*Art Weiss*)

Left: Outtake photo from *This Time We Mean It*, L-R: Gary Richrath, Michael Murphy, Neal Doughty, Alan Gratzer, Gregg Philbin (front). (*Henry Diltz, courtesy Illinois Rock and Roll Museum*)

The return of Kevin Cronin. REO in Kansas City, 1976. L to R: Gregg Philbin, Gary Richrath, Kevin Cronin. (*Courtesy Richard Galbraith*)

Left: A double LP retrospective, 1980's *Decade* collected tracks from the previous nine albums and added two new live recordings. (*Epic*)

Right: Released late 1980, *Hi Infidelity* was an international sensation and the biggest-selling album in the US in 1981. (*Epic*)

Left: 'Keep on Loving You' hit number one in the US and went top ten in Australia, Canada, and the UK. (*Epic*)

Right: Lyrics for Gary Richrath and Kevin Cronin's 'Lucky for You' from 1978's *Tuna Fish*. (*Illinois Rock and Roll Museum*)

Below: Gary Richrath's 'Take it on the Run' lyric sheet from 1980's *Hi Infidelity*. (*Illinois Rock and Roll Museum*)

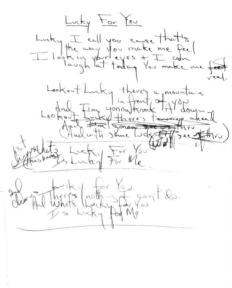

Right: Graham Lear filled the drum seat after Alan Gratzer retired. L-R: Graham Lear, Gary Richrath, Kevin Cronin, Neal Doughty, Bruce Hall. (*Dennis Keeley, courtesy Graham Lear*)

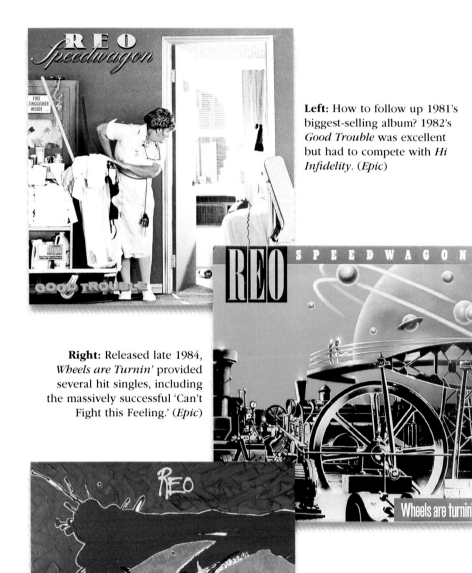

Left: How to follow up 1981's biggest-selling album? 1982's *Good Trouble* was excellent but had to compete with *Hi Infidelity*. (*Epic*)

Right: Released late 1984, *Wheels are Turnin'* provided several hit singles, including the massively successful 'Can't Fight this Feeling.' (*Epic*)

Left: *Life as We Know It*, from 1987, marked the end of the lineup of Cronin, Doughty, Gratzer, Hall, and Richrath. (*Epic*)

REO SPEEDWAGON
THE HITS

1. I DON'T WANT TO LOSE YOU
2. HERE WITH ME
3. ROLL WITH THE CHANGES
4. KEEP ON LOVING YOU
5. THAT AIN'T LOVE
6. TAKE IT ON THE RUN
7. IN MY DREAMS
8. DON'T LET HIM GO
9. CAN'T FIGHT THIS FEELING
10. KEEP PUSHIN'
11. TIME FOR ME TO FLY
12. ONE LONELY NIGHT
13. BACK ON THE ROAD AGAIN
14. RIDIN' THE STORM OUT

Above: *The Hits,* released in 1988, featured two new songs, the final recordings with Alan Gratzer and Gary Richrath. (*Epic*)

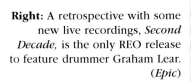

Left: 1990's *The Earth* was the last studio release on Epic, and the first with Dave Amato (guitar) and Bryan Hitt (drums). (*Epic*)

Right: A retrospective with some new live recordings, *Second Decade,* is the only REO release to feature drummer Graham Lear. (*Epic*)

Left: Richrath Band, early 1990s. After REO, Gary Richrath worked with Michael Jahnz (left) and his band Vancouver, touring and recording. (*Michael Jahnz*)

Below: REO in Germany, June 2008. L-R: Neal Doughty, Kevin Cronin, Dave Amato. (*Steven Mertes*)

'Back on the Road Again' in Germany, June 2008. L-R: Neal Doughty, Kevin Cronin, Bruce Hall, Dave Amato. (*Steven Mertes*)

Right: Early guitarist Steve Scorfina with Neal Doughty in St. Louis for radio station KSHE's 48th Birthday Party in 2015. (*Steve Scorfina*)

Left: REO on stage, 2018. L-R: Kevin Cronin, Bruce Hall, Dave Amato, Bryan Hitt. (*Art Weiss*)

Right: Kevin and Lisa Cronin performing 'In My Dreams' in 2022. (*Author*)

Left: Having been out of print, 1996's *Building the Bridge* was reissued in 2022, with a vinyl release in January 2023. (*Mailboat Records*)

Right: Most tracks on 1999's *The Ballads* were from the Epic years, with two newly-recorded songs added to the mix. (*Epic*)

Left: *Arch Allies* provided fans with a souvenir from the REO/Styx tour in 2000. The bands jammed together for the encores. (*CMC International*)

reospeedwagon
FIND YOUR OWN WAY HOME

Right: *Find Your Own Way Home*, from 2007, found producer Joe Vannelli playing keyboards on many tracks. (*Speedwagon Recordings*)

NOT SO SILENT NIGHT
CHRISTMAS WITH REO SPEEDWAGON

Left: REO's holiday offering, *Not So Silent Night*, was released in 2009 and rereleased in 2010 and 2017 with additional tracks. (*Rhino*)

Right: *Live at Moondance Jam*, taken from the band's 2010 show in Walker, Minnesota, was released in 2013. (*Frontiers*)

LIVE AT MOONDANCE JAM
DELUXE EDITION CD/DVD

Left: Original vocalist Terry Luttrell performing in the summer of 2022. Joe Council (left) and Terry Luttrell. (*Author*)

Below: The 2022 Illinois Rock and Roll Museum Induction Ceremony. Cronin, Amato, and Doughty perform American Breed's 'Bend Me, Shape Me.' (*Author*)

Right: The Illinois Rock and Roll Museum in Joliet featuring the band's live album. REO was inducted into the museum in 2021. (*Author*)

still had the tape. 'My recollection,' said Shepard, 'is that I gave away the only copy of that original (recording), gave it to Neal or Alan' at the Chicago show. The recording has never surfaced.

Momentum for the album continued to build and on 7 May 1981, the band made its first appearance on Britain's *Top of the Pops*. It was a video rather than an in-studio appearance, but nonetheless, REO were in the UK consciousness with 'Keep on Loving You.' A little over two months later, REO were back on *Top of the Pops*. Again, it was a video instead of an in-person appearance, this time for 'Take It on the Run.' The video aired twice, first on 23 July and a second time on 6 August.

In July 1981, REO headlined a show at Madison Square Garden in New York City. Around the time *R.E.O./T.W.O.* was released, Cronin told his parents that when REO became famous and played Madison Square Garden, he would fly them first-class to see it. It was meant mostly as a joke, but he kept his promise and his parents were there at the sold-out show. Other stops on the tour included Canada and the band's first visit to Japan.

By late 1981, the album had produced four hit singles and earned the distinction of being that year's biggest-selling record in the US. Another two songs were not released as singles but made it onto *Billboard*'s Mainstream Rock chart based on airplay. That same year, REO earned their first and only American Grammy nomination. It was an odd category, Best Rock Performance by a Duo or Group with Vocal, pitting albums (from REO, Foreigner, and The Rolling Stones) against singles (The Police and Stevie Nicks with Tom Petty and Heartbreakers). When the 24th Grammy Awards show was broadcast on 24 February 1982, REO lost to The Police's 'Don't Stand So Close to Me.'

In time, *Hi Infidelity* sold over 10,000,000 copies in the US, earned a silver award in the UK for sales of 60,000, and went five times platinum (500,000 sales for an album released before May 2008) in Canada. In the US, with REO's newfound success, *R.E.O./T.W.O.* was lifted to gold status (500,000), as was *Decade*. A diamond award for sales of 10,000,000 is part of the REO collection on display at the Illinois Rock and Roll Museum in Joliet, Illinois.

'Don't Let Him Go' (Cronin) (3:44)

Cronin wrote the album's opener based around a propulsive 'Bo-Diddley' style beat. As he was composing it, strumming the 'dun-dun-dun-*duuhn*-dah-dun-dun-dun' beat, his then-toddler son was dancing about the room. The line 'don't let him go' was based on that moment, with Cronin watching and originally singing, 'Go, baby, go.'

It begins with droning bass and guitar before Gratzer's primal beat comes in. Tension builds as Cronin sings the first two verses, then breaks loose with the chorus of 'Don't let him go.' Throughout, bass and drums provide a heavy foundation and drive the song without ever interfering. Doughty turns in a supercharged solo, and Richrath follows with a raunchy guitar break.

The intent behind the song is straightforward: men can be immature, self-absorbed idiots who have good intentions, women should be patient and not give up, the relationship will be worth it in the end. It served as a collective plea to the band members' wives and girlfriends. 'Don't Let Him Go' reached number 24 in the US and hit number 10 in Canada. It served as an ideal opening number on the concert setlist for many years.

'Keep on Loving You' (Cronin) (3:19)
Initially, Epic didn't even want this song on the album, believing it wasn't good enough. The band and management prevailed. REO's first number one single in the US, 'Keep on Loving You' was released several weeks before the album, offering a preview of *Hi Infidelity*. It went gold (sales of 1,000,000 pre-1988) in the US after a few months and eventually was certified platinum (2,000,000). The song made it to number 2 in Canada, 3 in Australia, and 7 in the UK, where it earned silver certification.

Cronin has never taken piano lessons and is sometimes needlessly self-deprecating about his keyboard skills. He wrote much of the song after waking in the middle of the night and sitting at the piano at his small home studio. The chorus wasn't yet written but later came to him when he played his new song for the rest of the band. Initially, the other band members were sceptical, feeling it was too soft.

Another song about relationships, it's telling the listener that even when the instinct is to run when things get rough, sometimes it's better to stick around and try to work it out. It begins with Cronin's piano, pulling in the listener and setting a 'ballad' tone. Emotion heightens during the initial verses, but with a completely different feel than the build-up of 'Don't Let Him Go.'

A beautiful, bluesy guitar solo scorches the more tender, pre-chorus part of the song, creating the 'power' in what came to be known as the power ballad. The band has joked that when Richrath crafted that solo, he was either trying to drown out Cronin's incessant playing of the unfinished song in the studio or was simply finding the right hard-edged sound to balance it.

With Cronin on piano, Doughty handles organ. Background vocals are by The He-Man Broken Hearts Club Choir (Kelly, Page, Cronin). Steve Forman, who helped with percussion on *Nine Lives*, returns for more.

The video created for the song is bookended by vignettes of Cronin talking to a psychiatrist. In between, footage of the band on stage is interspersed with the members lounging in a stark room with the same woman who played the psychiatrist. Just prior to the guitar solo, Doughty hands a telephone to her. She puts it to her ear, the camera follows the curly phone cord, and it's connected directly to Richrath's guitar, which speaks for him. It's a clever nod to the live version of '157 Riverside Avenue,' with 'somebody calling you up and talking to you with their guitar.'

The song became available as a downloadable track for *Rock Band* in February 2013. In 2021, basketball player Shaquille O'Neal sang 'Keep on Loving You' (while in the shower) in an automobile insurance commercial. When country music legend Dolly Parton decided to record the song for her 2023 *Rock Star* album, she turned it into a duet with Cronin, giving it a darker feel.

'Follow My Heart' (Richrath, Tom Kelly) (3:47)
Not counting 1974's 'Lost in a Dream,' which future member Hall co-wrote, REO didn't use outside songwriters until *Hi Infidelity*. They'd done several covers ('Little Queenie,' 'Without Expression,' 'Out of Control'), but originals had always come from the band. 'Follow My Heart' was written by Richrath and band associate Kelly.

The song's harder, darker sound contrasts nicely after the previous ballad. The wah-wah and echo give the guitar, and the entire song, an uncertainty somewhere between dream state and reality, between emotion and rational thought. Cronin offers strong, aggressive vocals. After the Crystal demos, when it came time to record 'Follow My Heart' for real, Richrath couldn't remember his original solo and had to refer back to the demo to relearn it.

'In Your Letter' (Richrath) (3:14)
After the heavier 'Follow My Heart' comes the 1950s doo-wop of 'In Your Letter.' It's reminiscent of The Ronettes or any girl group of that era and provides an uplifting, innocent vibe, though the subject is a Dear John letter. Theme-wise, it fits on the album. Stylistically, it was a musical jump but works extremely well. The song, which made the Top 20 in America, is based on an incident where the band returned home from a tour and Doughty found a note from his wife that she'd left him.

Richrath uses an electric 12-string guitar for the track. In the video, despite wearing long sleeves, he can be seen performing with a cast on his left arm, having broken his elbow not long before. Midway through, Doughty moves in with a piano solo he'd sketched out in his mind ahead of time, and which was done in a single take. Richrath's following chirpy guitar break is equally beautiful and memorable. The He-Man Broken Hearts Club Choir returns on background vocals, this time with additional member N. Yolletta (phonetically, 'in ya lettah').

'Take It on the Run' (Richrath) (3:59)
'Take It on the Run' is another example of how the Richrath/Cronin team produced exceptional music. It's a Richrath number, but Cronin is credited with 'lyrical assistance' for the 'take it on the run' line, among others. The original working title was 'Don't Let Me Down' or 'Don't Bring Me Down' (depending on the source of the story) and it's a ballad, which wasn't Richrath's usual territory. He and Cronin had been working on songs at Richrath's ranch in California when at the end of the day, Cronin asked if he had anything else. Richrath played a slow, country-style song he'd been working on. By the time the band was done with it, it was a rock song.

While 'Keep on Loving You' was more about perseverance and working through relationship troubles, 'Take It on the Run' was about ending things after hearing rumors, even if 'I don't believe it.' It was the second single from the album. Epic initially resisted, but as with 'Keep on Loving You,' band and management forced the move. The label certainly didn't think it would be a hit even after giving in. Despite the record company's lack of faith, the song made it to number 5 in the US, 4 in Canada, and 19 in the UK. 'Take It on the Run' became available for *Rock Band* in April 2009.

'Tough Guys' (Cronin) (3:48)

'Tough Guys' was based on a time from Cronin's childhood and is, at its core, an anti-bullying number. When he was 10 or 11 years old, he had to walk to and from music lessons. With his guitar case, he was often harassed by older kids. Things changed after The Beatles appeared on *The Ed Sullivan Show* on a Sunday night in America. After that, kids who previously had been tormenting him suddenly wanted to be in a band with him.

An audio clip from a 1937 *Little Rascals* (originally known as *Our Gang*) comedy short announces the song. Prior to making this album, Doughty fell asleep in front of the TV one night and awoke to a *Little Rascals* episode titled 'Hearts are Thumps' and quickly video-recorded it. The line, 'Say, Romeo, what happened to your promise to the He-Man Woman Haters Club?' serves as the inspiration for the naming of the He-Man Broken Hearts Club Choir and the Waspel Gospel He-Manettes, used for background vocals on several *Hi Infidelity* songs (though, oddly, not 'Tough Guys'). It was not released as a single, but still garnered significant airplay and made it to 25 on the US Rock chart.

'Out of Season' (Cronin, Tom Kelly) (3:05)

This is another of Kelly's earliest songwriting credits on an REO record, but he'd known the band since their days in Champaign. Over the next few albums, Kelly would author more than half a dozen songs for REO, often with writing partner Billy Steinberg.

'Out of Season' laments a lost chance at love after the narrator takes his girlfriend for granted. The track begins with layered guitars, Cronin then singing, 'I found out just a little too late.' Richrath's solo pierces and squeals, packing a weighty punch in a short 15 seconds. The chorus is smooth and rich, Cronin providing his own backing and harmony vocals. This was never a single, but as an album track, it received considerable airplay in the US, reaching number 59 on *Billboard*'s Top Tracks chart.

'Shakin' It Loose' (Richrath) (2:24)

This rocker is a Richrath number, though Cronin is credited with lyrical assistance, as he was with 'Take It on the Run.'

Clearly, the band had a good time recording this. In some ways, it matches the 1950s style of 'In Your Letter,' which may be why it was used as a B-side to that single, but with a Little Richard piano vibe. As Cronin shouts, 'Shake it loose,' Doughty takes the first solo on piano, a frisky run across the keys. Not to be outdone, Richrath plunges in with a noisy solo of his own, cranking away as Hall keeps it grounded on bass. Background vocals are provided by Cronin and Kelly. The track ends with a definitive 'brrrrmp' on Gratzer's drumkit. The song was sometimes used as an encore, its high spirits draining any remaining energy from the band and the audience.

'Someone Tonight' (Hall) (2:39)
After 'Back on the Road Again' from *Nine Lives*, fans expected at least one number on *Hi Infidelity* with Hall on lead vocals. 'Someone Tonight' is about the pursuit of love (or at least sex). It opens with guitars and drums building up to the first verse where Hall announces, 'You got it, I want it.' Cronin provides harmony vocals, flawlessly complementing Hall's voice. Doughty layers some synth under most of the track and Richrath slides in with fiery guitar after the second chorus. It's too bad it's not performed as often as 'Back on the Road Again,' though it was dusted off for the 2019 tour.

'I Wish You were There' (Cronin) (4:26)
This is a wistful, slightly melancholy tune evoking nostalgia, heartache, and hope. The bluesy feeling is a perfect way to wind down a powerful album after the emotional highs and uncertainties playing out across both sides of vinyl.
　　Doughty handles the Hammond organ, while Cronin plays piano and acoustic guitar. Richrath coaxes sweet notes from his guitar from the first to the last. Background vocals by The Waspel Gospel He-Manettes of Kelly, Page, and Cronin add to the richness of the track. In 2019, the song made a welcome return to the concert setlist.

Related Recordings
Hi Infidelity Then Again… Live! Sirius XM Artist Confidential Series (2007)
In 2006, the line-up of Doughty, Cronin, Hall, Amato, and Hitt celebrated the 25th anniversary of *Hi Infidelity* by performing the album in sequence for a theatre audience in Washington, DC, as part of satellite radio Sirius XM's *Artist Confidential Series*. The result showed how well the songs have held up and demonstrated how good the latter-day REO are.
　　When *Find Your Own Way Home* was released in 2007, a limited-edition set included the first official release of *Then Again… Live* on enhanced CD. There's no storytelling or chatter between the songs, just a straight-through rendition of the tracks. The enhanced CD included three performance videos from the show: 'Out of Season,' 'Someone Tonight,' and 'I Wish You were There.'

Hi Infidelity (30th Anniversary Edition) The Crystal Demos (2011)
The 'demos' were much more polished than what one would normally expect and more akin to rehearsals. At Crystal Studios, the band laid down basic

tracks, worked out overdubs and solos, and were still figuring out arrangements before heading into a better studio to record definitive versions of the songs. As most fans know, when the band later attempted the 'real' versions of the songs, they couldn't recreate the magic that was on those Crystal tapes. After many frustrating efforts, the band returned to the demos and ended up using them for much of the final record.

Then those demo tapes disappeared ... for more than 25 years. Eventually, they were discovered in their manager's garage and were restored in time for the 30th-anniversary edition of *Hi Infidelity*. The demo tapes have a slightly different running order than the final album, and 'Out of Season' doesn't appear. There's also a lack of keyboards on most of the tracks. 'Shakin' It Loose' is an instrumental here, and just as fun as the version with lyrics, though Doughty's piano is sorely missed. The addition of the demos on the anniversary edition of the CD makes it worth buying *Hi Infidelity* all over again.

Live & In Color Promos (1981)
Taken from the MTV Denver broadcast, two songs ('Keep on Loving You,' 'Don't Let Him Go') were distributed to radio stations as *Live & In Color*. Those, plus live recordings of 'Take It on the Run' (also from the Denver show) and 'In Your Letter,' are included in *The Classic Years 1978-1990*.

Related Tracks
'Lost in Carolina' (1981) [Unreleased]
Heavy Metal was a 1981 science fiction/fantasy adult animated film following the concept of the *Heavy Metal* graphic magazine, consisting of multiple short stories accompanied by music from acts such as Don Felder, Cheap Trick, and Sammy Hagar. In a 1981 interview with *Hit Parader*, Richrath stated the band had completed a song called 'Lost in Carolina' for the film and soundtrack, but it wasn't used and has never surfaced.

'Holly Would' by Richrath Band (Richrath) (1992)
'Holly Would' was intended to be on *Hi Infidelity*, but Richrath couldn't get the vocals worked out the way he wanted and shelved it. Once he began working on the *Only the Strong Survive* album, he resurrected it with Michael Jahnz and together, they got the sound Richrath was looking for.

The track begins on guitar. Dave Fraser's keyboards move in as Jahnz begins, 'I never met a woman who made me feel like Holly would.' It tells of walking away from the woman 'who made me feel like nobody could.' Jahnz's vocals convey the emotions of loss and regret, knowing it's too late to go back. Jahnz handles rhythm guitar. Midway through the track, Richrath plays a sharp, bluesy solo before the chorus returns. Then it's another solo, playing out through the fade, proving even after leaving REO, he was still the same brilliant musician fans loved. Had Richrath been able to finish it in 1980, the song would have been an excellent contribution to *Hi Infidelity*, but it's now hard to imagine anyone but Jahnz singing it.

'In Your Letter' by Richrath Band (Richrath) (1992)

As with 'Only the Strong Survive,' the band honors the REO version without becoming merely an imitation. The instrumental breaks are different and the song is about a minute longer than the original rendition. The arrangement is similar to *Hi Infidelity*'s, but still has its own identity. Fraser lets loose on a rollicking piano solo, answered by Richrath, who contributes new guitar work. Under it all, Tracy Martins (drums) and Jim Sorensen (bass) provide the foundation that keeps the track rocking along. Jahnz gives us an a cappella 'in your letter, oooh, in your letter' to end the song.

The Richrath Band's *Only the Strong Survive* is an overlooked gem that showed Richrath moving back toward a harder sound. After being out of print, it was rereleased in 2018.

Good Trouble (1982)

Personnel:
Kevin Cronin: lead vocals, rhythm guitar
Gary Richrath: lead guitar
Alan Gratzer: drums
Neal Doughty: keyboards
Bruce Hall: bass guitar
The Good Trouble Makers, The Powdertones, Richard Page, Tom Kelly: backing vocals
Producers: Kevin Cronin, Gary Richrath, Kevin Beamish, Alan Gratzer
Engineer: Kevin Beamish
Assistant Engineers: Bruce Barris, Tom Cummings
Record Label: Epic Records
Released: 11 June 1982
Running Time: 37:39
Highest Chart Place: US: 7, UK: 29

Released while *Hi Infidelity* was still on *Billboard*'s Top 200, *Good Trouble* is sometimes referred to as a rushed album and band members have stated they weren't prepared for it. The band had come off a massive tour with no time to enjoy their newfound success, but the pressure was on to craft another record as quickly as possible. Cronin, who contributed four tunes, has often said he felt he didn't have time to work out his songs, though most fans might disagree. Probably the biggest fault with this LP is that it had the task of following *Hi Infidelity*. Anything coming after that would be viewed as a disappointment, no matter how good the songwriting, performances, and sales. Had the chronological order of those two records been reversed, *Good Trouble* might have been seen as a triumph. When it came time to start the new record, the first day in the studio degenerated into disagreements and arguments, with no work accomplished. Fortunately, the sessions quickly improved. As opposed to the themes of infidelity and love gone wrong on the previous release, here, the songs are more about finding love and working on relationships.

The cover of the album is stylistically similar to *Hi Infidelity*, using the same photographer and art direction and design team. The image is inspired by a June 1957 Norman Rockwell painting titled 'Just Married (Hotel Maids and Confetti).' Here, someone from a cleaning crew stands looking into a trashed hotel room. The lettering for the band's name and the album title are in similar positions on the cover. The fonts are not identical, but close enough to remind anyone picking up the album that this is the same band. The back cover shows REO outside the closed door of room 1914, perhaps a nod to the early years of the Speed Wagon for which they were named. By most accounts, the Speed Wagon vehicle didn't come into production until 1915 but was being developed in 1914.

The inner sleeve features credits and individual musician photos on one side, with lyrics on the reverse side. The photos have a 1950s teen idol appearance to them. The paper label in the center of the vinyl LP is a photo of plexiglass door handles, perhaps to indicate good trouble awaits anyone who enters.

After working with outside writer Kelly on *Hi Infidelity*, the band kept all songwriting in-house, but Kelly and Page (background vocals), and Forman (percussion) all return. The team of Kelly, Page, and Cronin also found time in 1983 to appear on Survivor's *Caught in the Game*, providing backing vocals. Although Beamish was back for another turn as a producer, he departed before the record was finished and wasn't involved in REO's next album.

Promotion included an MTV 30-minute documentary, *The Good Trouble Sessions*, about making videos for the album's songs. REO also appeared on BBC's *The Old Grey Whistle Test* on 15 April 1983 with concert footage from Germany's *Rock Pop in Concert*. The show at Metro Arena in Rockford, Illinois, was recorded for Westwood One radio in the US. Two songs from that broadcast, 'Keep the Fire Burnin'' and 'Roll with the Changes,' later appeared on *The Second Decade of Rock and Roll 1981 to 1991*. The tour included a few stops in Europe, though most dates were in the US. The setlist variously included: 'Good Trouble,' 'Let's Be-Bop,' 'Girl with the Heart of Gold,' 'Back in My Heart Again,' 'Keep the Fire Burnin',' 'Stillness of the Night,' 'I'll Follow You,' and 'The Key.' Since then, *Good Trouble* songs have rarely been played in concert.

The album didn't come near matching *Hi Infidelity*'s overwhelming success, but still climbed to number 7 in the US and sold more than a million copies, earning platinum status. It made it to 18 in Canada and reached the Top 40 in the UK. It didn't find the huge audience its predecessor did, but anyone who dismissed this album upon its release missed out on seriously good music.

'Keep the Fire Burnin'' (Cronin) (3:53)

The first single, 'Keep the Fire Burnin'' was released a few weeks before the album and boded well, making it to the Top 10 in both the US and Canada. Cronin wrote it on piano after a bout of writer's block and though it was a hit, he's said it felt incomplete. The song, about working through a tough patch in a relationship, brings to mind 'Roll with the Changes' with its organ, piano, and attitude. It's energetic and uplifting, urging 'we can never give up' and 'keep looking for the good.'

Cronin works the piano while Doughty handles organ. Midway through, Doughty takes flight, dancing across the keys while Gratzer and Hall never let up. After the last verse, Cronin pounds away on piano, building tension before turning it over to Richrath. Richrath rips into a solo, cutting through as the 'keep the fire burnin'' line is repeated. Background vocals are provided by The Good Trouble Makers of Cronin, Kelly, and Page. Also joining is Forman on percussion.

Despite making it to 7 in the US (and being particularly popular in Puerto Rico), it did not appear later on *The Hits*. It did make it onto 2004's *The*

Essential REO Speedwagon. Cronin eventually brought it back into the setlist at times years later as an acoustic number with a few revised chords.

'Sweet Time' (Cronin) (3:08)
Intentional or not, *Good Trouble* seemed to mimic the initial template of *Tuna Fish* to some extent. If 'Keep the Fire Burning" had a 'Roll with the Changes' feel to it, 'Sweet Time' follows with an acoustic beginning, the same way 'Time for Me to Fly' followed 'Roll with the Changes.' Coincidentally, the first two songs on *Tuna Fish* and on *Good Trouble* were the first two singles released from each album, in the same order.

This one eases in on acoustic guitar, the music matching the emotion of the lyrics. Cronin wrote it in the wake of *Hi Infidelity*, when everything was moving too fast and life was nearly out of control. There's a fragile uncertainty at the start of the song, a hope that things might slow down enough to enjoy the moment and contemplate life's next moves. When the first chorus comes around, the uncertainty is gone, replaced by confidence and a sense of making things right after any wrongs. Following the second chorus, Richrath steps in with a rich guitar sound, in keeping with the mood. Background vocals are by the same trio as on 'Keep the Fire Burnin',' though this time, they called themselves The Powdertones. Percussionist Forman plays chimes and crotales (best described as small disks arranged in a row like a keyboard and struck with a small mallet).

Similar to his feelings about 'Keep the Fire Burnin',' Cronin has always felt 'Sweet Time' wasn't complete when they recorded it. The single made it to number 26 in the US.

'Girl with the Heart of Gold' (Hall) (4:24)
One of two songs on this album by Hall, he shares lead vocal duties with Cronin. They take turns on the verses and together work the chorus. The band hadn't shared lead vocal duties like this since 1976's *R·E·O*. The title sums up the song about a man finding the woman of his dreams. He knows how fortunate he is and promises always to do right by her.

'Girl with the Heart of Gold' has a harder edge than the tracks preceding it. Stylistically, it begins with a beat similar to the start of The Ronettes' 'Be My Baby' (*dah, dah-dah*, boom, *dah, dah-dah*, boom) though all similarities end there. There's a nice, fat bass sound pushing the track as Hall begins, 'Night and day, day and night.' Richrath's gritty guitar punctuates the verses and breaks out for a solo about two-thirds of the way through. Kelly and Page return on backing vocals, this time without a collective name for themselves.

'Every Now and Then' (Richrath) (4:00)
'Every Now and Then' starts with a light, playful piano touch. The first several lines of lyrics begin with 'every now and then,' each line bringing back a

memory of that one past love, and 'every now and then' really meaning 'every minute of every day.'

Hall does a brief walk partway down the neck of his bass between the first and second verse. After the second verse, the band enters in full, but the tune maintains a lighter touch. Although that one special love has ended, the lyrics are hopeful for a reconciliation. Richrath draws a warm guitar tone, conveying both the loss and the optimism of reconnecting with that love. As the song winds down, Richrath winds up, wailing and soaring, squeezing in as much soloing as possible. Cronin, Kelly, and Page again handle background vocals, this time as The Trouble Makers.

'I'll Follow You' (Richrath) (4:24)
The last song on side one of the vinyl record, 'I'll Follow You' bursts in, proudly stomping along. It's the tale of a late-night chance encounter by a man and woman at a café in Texas, both parties uncertain of what they're looking for or where they're metaphorically headed, but happy to go there together.

After setting the scene over several verses, the chorus strikes and the woman in question makes the decision to go along with her newfound friend: 'She said, 'I'll follow, I'll follow you on your dare'.' Cronin delivers a meaty vocal and Doughty pounds along on piano like something out of a Texas roadhouse. This song deserves to be played over and over if only for Doughty's rapid-fire piano, like the previous album's 'Shakin' It Loose.' Not be outdone, when the time comes, Richrath picks up the challenge and riffs away on guitar for the final minute as the tune fades.

'The Key' (Cronin) (3:26)
'The Key' launches side two of the LP. The song is reflective of life in the wake of the massive success the band had finally achieved. Cronin has said that success didn't solve his problems. If anything, it magnified the faults: 'I left so much behind to find the dream that I was chasin'.' The song is about examining the turmoil and taking responsibility for one's own life, not waiting for or blaming others. The message, that it's important to look at the good and bad in yourself, is wrapped in an irresistible tune.

Forman is on shakers, helping on percussion again. Mid-song, Doughty plays a sparkling piano break before the band returns for another chorus. The tail end of the song belongs to Richrath's brief, sweet solo.

'Back in My Heart Again' (Richrath) (3:19)
The third of four songs by Richrath on *Good Trouble*, this one has an unusual cadence to the verses, the words of the verses almost clipped in staccato fashion. The lyrics tell of longing for an old girlfriend after breaking it off with her. The singer admits being wrong and regrets what happened, while pondering what it might take to win her back.

Cronin and Richrath work together through the verses, providing that REO acoustic/electric combination. Cronin serves as backup singer to himself, adding a richness to the chorus. Richrath makes a similar move with his solo, layering electric guitars, climbing one over another.

'Let's Be-Bop' (Hall) (3:14)

A Hall tune, here he writes a loosely autobiographical tale about the climb to the top and how great it feels to be performing in front of the thousands of fans who 'gave us the glory.' He knows it's best to enjoy the good times while they last and 'later on when it's over, we will think of you.' For the moment, though, all that matters is getting on stage and be-bopping.

Without overthinking it, this might be considered a follow-up to 'Find My Fortune' from 1973's *Ridin' the Storm Out*, about pursuing 'crazy dreams' and chasing stardom. Hall handles the lead vocals. Hall has stated in multiple interviews that the 'be-bop' title of the song is regrettable and he would've preferred something like 'Let's Rock.'

'Stillness of the Night' (Richrath) (3:43)

Another song of lost love, Richrath writes of the shock when realizing 'you're never coming back.' The Cronin/Richrath acoustic/electric pairing creates a solid foundation. After the second chorus, Doughty takes center stage, tearing into a synthesizer solo. Later, Richrath delivers a screaming solo, heading into darkness and shattering the stillness of the night.

'Good Trouble' (Cronin) (4:08)

It's not a love song, and it's not about lamenting lost love, either. The title track to the album is a rocker about hooking up after a show and having no regrets. It's all about getting into 'good trouble all night.'

Richrath piles on great riffs again and again, tearing into his guitar and creating his own good trouble. The song is a solid ending to the album and proves that even if the band felt they weren't ready when they recorded this, they still came out with a winner.

Related Recordings
'Johnny B. Goode' (Chuck Berry) 1985 [Unreleased]

REO's take on 'Johnny B. Goode' was an encore during some of their *Good Trouble* shows. A May 1983 Westwood One radio broadcast captured the song from a performance in Milwaukee, Wisconsin. Considering how much the band were enjoying themselves, it's a wonder they didn't consider the song for *Good Trouble*, especially if they were having trouble coming up with material for it. It would've created an REO/Chuck Berry trifecta, the band already having covered 'Little Queenie' and 'Rock and Roll Music.'

The performance is high-energy. Richrath's guitar burns it up, Doughty's piano just plain rocks, and Gratzer's drumming never tires. Cronin throws in scat vocals, singing 'go, John, Johnny, go, go, Johnny' atop Hall's climbing and descending bass lines. This recording was only ever available as part of the promotional radio broadcast, though a different 'Johnny B. Goode' live recording surfaced several years later.

'Blues Breaker (Dedicated to E.C.)' by Brian May + Friends (Brian May, Eddie Van Halen, Gratzer, Phil Chen, Fred Mandel) (1983)
A mini-LP that was a jam between friends, *Star Fleet Project* consisted of three songs performed by Brian May, Eddie Van Halen, Phil Chen, Fred Mandel, and REO's Gratzer, recorded on 21 and 22 April 1983 (Queen's Roger Tayler provided backing vocals at a later date). At the time, Gratzer and May were neighbors in Hancock Park in Los Angeles. The three songs clock in under 30 minutes: 'Star Fleet,' written by Paul Bliss for the UK sci-fi program of the same name and arranged by Brian May; 'Let Me Out,' written by May; and 'Blues Breaker,' a nearly 13-minute instrumental jam written and performed by all five musicians. The project was 'just for fun', and the 'E.C.' in the title was Eric Clapton.

The musicians are having a good time on 'Blues Breaker.' There's no pressure, just the joy of playing. It settles into a blues groove at the start, the laid-back feeling carrying through to the end. There's no drum solo, but Gratzer effortlessly shoulders guitars and piano to keep the music flowing and ends the jam with a mighty crash on cymbals. Though it was not intended for commercial issue, when it was released, it enjoyed a short stay on the charts, climbing to 125 in the US, 35 in the UK, and 69 in Canada. May stated an intent to release an expanded version of *Star Fleet Project*, with every take of every song and other bits from the studio, sometime in 2023.

Wheels are Turnin' (1984)

Personnel:
Kevin Cronin: lead vocals, rhythm guitar
Gary Richrath: lead guitar
Alan Gratzer: drums
Neal Doughty: keyboards
Bruce Hall: bass guitar
Tom Kelly, Richard Page, Tommy Funderburk: backup vocals
Steve Forman: percussion, congas, shakers on 'Thru the Window,' 'Live Every Moment,' 'Wheels are Turnin"
Bill Cuomo: orchestration on 'Can't Fight this Feeling'
Producers: Cronin, Richrath, Gratzer
Engineer and Production Assistant: David DeVore
Assistant Engineer: Julian Stoll
Record Label: Epic Records
Released: 5 November 1984
Running Time: 39:13
Highest Chart Place: US: 7, UK: –

After the relative disappointment of the million-selling *Good Trouble*, REO came out on top with *Wheels are Turnin'*. By this time, several band members had started making lifestyle changes, focusing on their health and pouring their energies into the music. The result was a US Top 10 album, with four Top 40 singles, that spent 49 weeks on the charts, twice as long as *Good Trouble*. Coincidentally, the band spent about twice as long crafting *Wheels are Turnin'* (eight months) as they did *Good Trouble* (about four months).

With producer Beamish leaving after *Good Trouble*, David DeVore was brought in. DeVore had previously been pursued for *Nine Lives* but wasn't available at the time. 'Can't Fight this Feeling' delivered a second number one single in the US and was the first REO single to hit number 1 in Canada ('Keep on Loving You' had peaked at two). While the single also made the Top 20 in the UK, the album failed to chart.

The record's front cover artwork depicted multiple wheels, from a steam engine to rings around a planet. The back cover featured a photo of the band. Rather than have a side one and side two, the center label of the vinyl record showed side A and side Z. The cassette, however, showed the traditional sides one and two. The inner sleeve showcased lyrics and music credits on one side, with production credits and a 'stereoscopic wheel' with images of the band on the other. Instructions for viewing the wheel invited consumers to cut it out from the sleeve, poke a needle through the center, and spin it in front of a mirror to watch the band members move, similar to a page flip cartoon. It was a literal way to engage the *Wheels are Turnin'* theme.

If some fans were disappointed by *Good Trouble*, it meant they might be reluctant to dive into *Wheels are Turnin'* and REO had to prove themselves again. In retrospect, some discontent within the band may have started to foment, but it isn't evident in the finished product. The performances are excellent and rock as hard as anything the band had done in the past.

Like much of the *Hi Infidelity* tour, Survivor opened many shows for REO. In addition to dates in the continental US, the tour found the band in Puerto Rico, Canada, Germany, Switzerland, England, Scotland, Ireland, and Japan. At London's Hammersmith Odeon, REO were joined during the 'Johnny B. Goode' encore by Brian May, John Entwistle, and Alvin Lee. At the inaugural Rock am Ring (Rock at the Ring) at Nürburgring in 1985, REO played 'Can't Fight this Feeling,' 'Live Every Moment,' and '157 Riverside Avenue' in front of a crowd estimated at 75,000.

REO appeared on the American TV program *Sold Gold* twice, first with 'I Do' Wanna Know' at the end of 1984, then later with 'Can't Fight this Feeling' in early 1985. Both performances were lip-synched. 1985 also found them lip-syncing 'Time for Me to Fly' on German television's *EinsFestival WWF Club*. In May 1985, the band performed at the Montreux Golden Rose Pop Festival. Footage of 'One Lonely Night' made its way onto the BBC's highlights from the festival, as part of *The Montreux Rock Festival: Part 4*.

The band's largest audience ever was their morning appearance in Philadelphia for the Live Aid famine relief benefit concert in July 1985, with close to 100,000 in attendance at JFK Stadium and 1.9 billion more watching on television. The event was set up with a revolving stage to avoid any downtime between acts. There was no sound check. When REO's time came, Doughty said in a 2015 interview with *NYS Music* that he started 'Can't Fight this Feeling' on piano, but the band couldn't hear themselves and assumed the sound wasn't being broadcast. That wasn't the case, but explains why Doughty had a false start, then began again. REO were limited to 10 minutes and performed two songs, the second being 'Roll with the Changes.' After Live Aid, the band had a show that night in Milwaukee, Wisconsin, a flight of about 700 miles. Due to weather, the band had to land in Chicago and take a bus to Milwaukee, getting to the show on time but making for a very long day.

It was on the *Wheels are Turnin'* tour in 1985, on the flight to Stockholm, Sweden, that the band Hotel Bill and the Incidentals came to be. The Incidentals consisted primarily of REO's road crew who had already been performing at soundchecks, and who were then tasked to be an official opening act at the Royal Opera House in Stockholm. While Hotel Bill was always Brad 'Porque' (pronounced porky) Baker, who worked as a guitar technician and much more for the band, The Incidentals' line-up changed over time but did include both Doughty and Cronin. Setlists consisted of classic rock tunes and originals.

Gratzer and Doughty also took time in 1984 to perform on Spirit's *Spirit of '84* (titled *The Thirteenth Dream* in the UK). Then in 1985, Doughty also played on Randy California's 'Restless Nights' from his album *Restless*. Doughty's work also showed up on California's 'Restless Nights (Instrumental)' from the *Jack Rabbit* 12-inch single. In February of 1986, Cronin appeared at the Vietnam Veterans Benefit concert in Los Angeles to perform 'Roll with the Changes.' About a month later, BBC 1 Wales *Late Night in Concert* aired 30 minutes of an REO concert filmed at Kansas City Kemper Arena in 1985. The band played 'Don't Let Him Go,' 'Take It on the Run,' 'Can't Fight this Feeling,' 'Shakin' It Loose,' 'Keep on Loving You,' 'Keep Pushin',' and 'Time for Me to Fly.'

Wheels are Turnin' reached number 7 in the US and in October 1990, was awarded double platinum status. In Canada, it hit number 15 and earned a platinum award.

'I Do' Wanna Know' (Cronin) (4:12)
The first track was also the first single, reaching 29 in the US and 52 in Canada, though it didn't dent the UK charts. 'I Do' Wanna Know,' from the song's title to the music itself, displays a sense of humor. It's a fast-moving, fun-loving boogie rock number. Radio programmers were probably expecting a ballad, which may explain why REO chose this as the first single.

The track harkens back to harder-rocking numbers, starting with a sharp riff from Richrath before the entire band jumps in and Cronin starts the first verse. The mid-song instrumental break arrives with a chunky organ solo, Doughty stabbing and rolling across the keys, taking the energy level even higher before turning it over to Richrath for some tasty guitar and a few more verses. After an abrupt false ending around the three-minute mark, another instrumental break kicks off, this time with Richrath first letting loose on his Gibson before Doughty returns on organ. Cronin, Page and Kelly handle the backing vocals.

To promote the song, REO made their quirkiest, most involved video ever, with animation, cartoonish sets, band member appearances as homemakers, rock stars, parents, naval officers, baseball players, and much more in the mix. It was directed by Sherry Revord and Kevin Dole, with Dole starring as the rebellious lead character. American comedian and actor Jim Varney ('KnowWhutIMean, Vern?') also appeared as an angel. Although the lyrics are about questioning a lover's faithfulness ('Just don't tell me that you love me, 'cause I don't wanna know'), the cheeky video is about a slightly out-of-control son who doesn't want to hear how much his family loves him. The son eventually ends up in hell, getting his appropriate rewards.

Director Revord happened to be an old girlfriend of Cronin's from their very young days and had married Dole. It was Revord who contacted Cronin and put things in motion. The video had a similar style to a short film Dole had made with Marion Kramer a few years earlier titled *Once Upon a Time*. It was a slight risk for the band, as Revord and Dole had directed only one music video (George Clinton's 'Last Dance') previously, but the results garnered a *Billboard* nomination for 'Best Performance, Group,' and four additional nominations from the US National Academy of Video Arts and Sciences for costumes, set design, performance by a music group, and direction. The video did not win in any category.

On the *Wheels are Turnin'* vinyl album front cover promotional sticker, the back cover, inner sleeve, and paper center label of the vinyl record; the song's title is listed as 'I Dowanna Know' though the picture sleeve for the single shows it as 'I Do' wanna Know.' In a July 1985 Creem interview, Cronin said the title started as 'I DoWanna Know' but should officially be 'I Do'Wanna Know.'

'One Lonely Night' (Doughty) (3:20)

'One Lonely Night' was the third single released from the album and, unusually, was not written by either Cronin or Richrath. It was Doughty who penned this one. He came up with the melody, recorded a basic track for himself, and kept playing it in his car while driving around Los Angeles until he had lyrics.

The mid-tempo tune begins on acoustic guitar, creating a pensive atmosphere as Cronin sets the scene with, 'You and your baby had some words today.' The song tells of a couple having an argument, where the man refuses to give in regardless of who's at fault, making for 'one lonely night.' Synthesizer underlies the verses and a scalding guitar solo hits before the final verse and chorus. Cronin shares backing vocals with Tommy Funderburk. Funderburk has worked with Eddie Money, Richard Marx, and even Spinal Tap. After singing on 'One Lonely Night,' Funderburk returned for the new songs on *The Hits*.

The accompanying video was created by Revord and Dole, the same team who directed 'I Do' Wanna Know.' The video adds levity to the song. It starts with a medieval flair, fife (or synthesizer) setting the tone as a knight returns home to domestic strife before announcing, 'I'm going... out.' Dole takes the lead character role of the knight, and the theme is similar to 'I Do' Wanna Know.' Here, the knight goes in search of Cronin's Merlin character, who transports the knight from medieval to modern times. The entire band plunges into their roles as waitress, bum, prostitutes, pimp, cops, and more. In the end, the knight returns to his love, having learned his lesson. 'One Lonely Night' peaked at 19 in the US and 35 in Canada. It did not make the UK charts.

'Thru the Window' (Hall, Jeffrey B. Hall) 5:01

Bassist Hall wrote 'Thru the Window' with his brother Jeffrey. Cronin, rather than Hall, sings lead vocals. Hall isn't even credited with background vocals, instead letting Cronin, Kelly, and Page handle the task. In 'Thru the Window,' the song's young protagonist slips out of his house through the window on a summer night, sneaking through neighborhoods to meet his girlfriend. She slips out her window to meet him and together, they run free, emotions fueling their flight.

Thick bass notes and chirpy synthesizer start the song. The synth has a 1980s feel, but Richrath's searing guitar provides contrast with its 1970s tone. Forman helps on percussion, as he has with many REO songs. The guitar flowing through the song is truly inspired and Richrath simply can't contain the heat as he burns through the latter half of the tune.

81

'Rock 'n' Roll Star' (Richrath, Cronin, Tom Kelly) 3:40

'Rock 'n' Roll Star' reflects on what follows after finally making it big in the business. After many earlier tunes told of the hard work on the climb to success, this one reflects on life now that they've achieved what they set out to do. Cronin sings about throwing 'my Fender in an old friend's car, I knew I'd come back as a rock 'n' roll star' but then being eaten alive by the press after succeeding. Instead of basking in the limelight, the band still have to prove and defend themselves.

Cronin works the acoustic counterpart to Richrath's electric guitar. Doughty's having fun, keyboards swelling and swirling between and under the verses and chorus. Hall and Gratzer's rhythm section hauls like a diesel engine. Richrath throws down rock star riffs and jams away, taking no prisoners. After all is said and done, despite the stress and pressure and endless touring, 'I still wanna be a rock 'n' roll star.'

'Live Every Moment' (Cronin) (4:56)

Following the raucousness of 'Rock 'n' Roll Star,' 'Live Every Moment' is buoyant and light but never trivial. There's no hidden meaning, no metaphor lurking in the lyrics, just a straightforward, heartfelt message that life is short and every day is a gift. This was the fourth Top 40 single from the album. Cronin wrote it during a break in Molokai, Hawaii, after the *Good Trouble* tour. It came to him while walking along the beach ('footprints in the sand, washed away without a warning'), which is probably why it conveys that sunny, breezy feeling.

The tune is uplifting and exuberant, Forman's congas and Doughty's relentless, lively piano lifting the mood even higher. Cronin, Page, Kelly, and Funderburk give a boost on backing vocals. Richrath rips into some excellent soloing in the second half of the song, adding an edge and urgency to the plea to 'live every moment, love every day.'

'Can't Fight this Feeling' (Cronin) 4:54

Titled 'You're My Guiding Light' during its earliest drafts, the second single from *Wheels are Turnin'* became REO's second US number one and achieved gold certification. It also hit number 1 and earned gold status in Canada, and 16 in the UK (also gold). Although it spent fewer weeks on the US charts than 'Keep on Loving You,' it was a bigger hit, sitting at number 1 for three weeks versus a single week for 'Keep on Loving You.' If the band hadn't been so rushed on *Good Trouble*, this track might've come to fruition earlier and been part of that album.

Cronin wrote the song on the piano and in some ways, it's a follow-up to 'Keep on Loving You.' He worked out three verses back in 1974 or 1975 during his break from REO but couldn't come up with the chorus. When revisiting the tune for *Wheels are Turnin'*, he'd planned to work with Eric Carmen (Raspberries, solo) but, at the last minute, had to back out due to illness and finished it on his own. The ballad is about starting out as friends but wanting more. After resisting the pull of love, Cronin sings of finally finding the courage to express what's been there all along. His vocals are passionate, the chorus swelling into something mighty and powerful.

Unlike many of Cronin's songs that feature piano, this time, he turned the keys over to Doughty. For the synthesizer orchestration, it was producer DeVore who brought in Bill Cuomo. Cuomo has worked with artists such as Don Henley and Mark Knopfler and has written songs with Steve Perry. Devore first recorded Cuomo's piece and then presented it to the band for their approval. Richrath again puts the power in the ballad, sawing and bending the notes, sending the track soaring. It's a love song, but there's nothing soppy in his performance.

UK retailers John Lewis & Partners and Waitrose & Partners used the song as part of their 2019 holiday promotions in a two-and-a-half-minute advertisement. Dan Smith, from Bastille, recorded the big production 'Can't Fight this Feeling' with the London Contemporary Orchestra for the 'Excitable Edgar' advertisement. Although it sounds like Smith sings the opening line as 'I *don't* fight this feeling,' that's apparently a production quirk and not a mis-sung word. Bastille recorded and released the song the same year on their *Doom Days (This Got Out of Hand)*, with their version reaching 39 in the UK.

This might be the REO song most featured in TV and films. It's popped up in everything from *It's Always Sunny in Philadelphia* (Season 15) and *Stranger Things* (Season 3) to *Horton Hears a Who!* (2008) and *Penguins* (2019). It was also covered on *Glee* (Season 1). This was Cronin's mother's favorite REO song. During a November 2016 REO concert, Cronin brought his mother Millie, aka 'Mother Rock,' on stage and sang it to her. 'Can't Fight this Feeling' is also Bruce and Kimmie Hall's special song.

'Gotta Feel More' (Richrath, Cronin, Tom Kelly) (4:26)
The team of Richrath, Cronin, and Kelly wrote two songs for this record. 'Gotta Feel More' starts with a strong beat and piercing guitar and rocks from the first note to the last while it reaches for more.

The lyrics point in two different directions. First, the song's protagonist is in love and because of that, he's experiencing everything with heightened awareness. His partner is showing him there's much more out there in life than what they already have and together, they're going to experience everything. Conversely, the lines 'I still love you to the core, I just gotta feel more' make it seem like now he knows the only way to experience more of life is to leave her behind. It's time to say goodbye and go in search of more. With about three-quarters of the lyric lines beginning either 'I' or 'I've,' it's a safe bet the protagonist is thinking of himself more than his girlfriend.

Cronin's forceful vocals add to the song's hard edge while drums and guitar drive the song. The first instrumental break comes midway through and brings more, more, more guitar, with Richrath wringing out a screaming solo.

After Cronin returns with the chorus and howls, 'I just gotta feel more,' Richrath launches another hard-biting solo, notes ringing in the listener's ears after the fadeout.

'Break His Spell' (Richrath) (2:57)

'Break His Spell' is Richrath's only solo songwriting credit on *Wheels are Turnin'*, but rather than being drenched in electric guitar, the track shimmers with crisp keyboards. Doughty's piano carries this up-tempo tune, about competing for the affection of a woman. The lyrics tell of working to win her back after taking her for granted and letting her slip away.

The musical tone is similar to *Hi Infidelity*'s 'In Your Letter' from four years earlier, which Richrath also wrote, with sparkling piano and background vocals leaning toward that 1950s sound. Not quite two-thirds of the way through, Doughty takes flight. He tickles and teases the keys, traveling up and down the board, then cascading back for the final verse. The shortest track on the album, 'Break His Spell' served as the B-side to 'Can't Fight This Feeling.'

'Wheels are Turnin'' (Cronin) (5:47)

Over the years, Cronin has been associated with ballads more than rockers, but he's written as many of the latter as the former. This is one of those rockers and is a near-perfect track. A statement of the band's collective mindset at the time, the song is about getting back on track to where they wanted to be professionally and personally. After struggling in the wake of unimaginable success, Cronin sings, 'The thrill's returning.'

The song wastes no time, attacking from the start with drums, guitar, bass, and piano. As Doughty pounds the piano over Hall's locomotive bass lines, Richrath tosses off a few wicked riffs before Cronin begins the first verse. He reflects on how life has been and decides it's time to make changes and move on. Thematically, this could be considered an extension of 'Keep Pushin',' telling regardless of how difficult and stagnant things may get, one can dig deep and move forward again.

After Cronin sings, 'I get out of control, I can't hold on to the brakes,' Doughty rips into a rapid-fire piano solo. Following another chorus or two, Richrath is there with some vicious guitar, clawing away at the strings as 'Wheeeeels are turnin'' repeats until the hard ending. At close to six minutes, 'Wheels are Turnin'' is the longest on the album. It was the flipside to 'One Lonely Night.' Every fan should be familiar with this tune.

Related Tracks
'Johnny B. Goode' (Chuck Berry) 1985 (4:02)

After covering two Chuck Berry songs on their studio albums, 'Johnny B. Goode' turned up as an encore during the *Good Trouble* tour, and again occasionally on the *Wheels are Turnin'* tour. Richrath kicks off the tune with raunchy riffs before drums, bass, and keyboards join in, all as raucous as the guitar. Doughty is in top form, flying across the piano, hammering away, gliding up and down the keys. This recording was from a January 1985 show and appeared on Epic/Legacy's 2010 *Setlist: The Very Best of REO Speedwagon LIVE*, as well as the *Live 1980-1990* disc from *Classic Years 1978-1990*.

'Wherever You're Goin' (It's Alright)' (Cronin) (*The Goonies: Original Motion Picture Soundtrack*) 1985 (5:00)
REO contributed this song to *The Goonies*, a comedy adventure about kids following a treasure map in hopes of saving their homes from foreclosure. It's an optimistic 'kids film' track, with lyrics like, 'Say goodbye, look to the sky, set your course on into the night.' The band performed 'Time for Me to Fly' and 'Wherever You're Goin' (It's Alright)' at Westfalenhalle in Dortmund as part of German television program *Peter's Pop Show* in 1985. The audience was live, but the performances were mimed. As with *Wheels are Turnin,'* 'Wherever You're Goin' (It's Alright)' was produced by David DeVore. Initially available only on *The Goonies* soundtrack, it later appeared on *Best Foot Forward*, and in 1988 was the B-side of 'Here with Me' from *The Hits*.

'Wasted Rock Ranger' by Hotel Bill and the Incidentals (Brad Baker) [Unreleased]
Hotel Bill and the Incidentals played many shows but never settled down and made a proper album. 'Wasted Rock Ranger' was written by Porque Baker and serves as a theme song for the troupe of rotating musicians. It provides a teaser for the kind of music the band played: irreverent, fun, and catchy, served atop incredible, solid musicianship. The tune has a backwoods flavor, with hayseed attitude and a hoe-down feel, guaranteed to serve up a good time. American band Great White covered 'Wasted Rock Ranger' on 1989's *Twice Shy*. The lyrics are humourous hyperbole, but doubtless rooted in reality: 'I have beenies with the breakfast toast, quaaludes with the evening roast.'

Life as We Know It (1987)

Personnel:
Neal Doughty: keyboards
Alan Gratzer: drums
Gary Richrath: lead guitar, rhythm guitar
Kevin Cronin: lead vocals, rhythm guitar, acoustic guitar
Bruce Hall: bass guitar, lead vocals on 'Accidents Can Happen'
Steve Forman: percussion
Bob Carlisle, Tom Kelly, Julia Waters, Maxine Waters, Terry Wood: backing vocals
Producers: Cronin, Richrath, Gratzer, David DeVore
Engineer: David DeVore
Assistant Engineer: Julian Stoll
Record Label: Epic Records
Released: February 1987
Running Time: 40:19
Highest Chart Place: US: 28, UK: –

REO's twelfth studio album was forged during another rough time in some of the band members' personal lives. Cronin was working his way through divorce and Richrath was unhappy in the band. After three songwriting credits on 'Wheels are Turning,' this time, the guitarist turned in two songs to Cronin's six. Doughty and Hall wrote one each.

Before making *Life as We Know It*, the band was approached to be part of what eventually became one of the biggest films and soundtracks of 1986: *Top Gun*. Very early in the creative process, REO were offered a chance to record 'Danger Zone' for the movie but passed on it. When the Giorgio Moroder/Tom Whitlock track was presented, it was a bare-bones demo, with nothing more than a synthesizer running through the track. There was no accompanying vocal, just a lyric sheet and an early copy of the film script. The lead (Tom Cruise) hadn't yet been cast. Additionally, REO would not have been allowed to contribute any original tracks. Based on what little the band had to go on, it's not surprising they turned it down. Ultimately, Kenny Loggins recorded it.

Despite the turmoil behind the scenes, outwardly *Life as We Know It* still gave the fans great songs and strong performances. The album produced three hit singles, with two entering the US Top 20. The album cover was a colorful piece by Donald Ryan. The inner sleeve had lyrics on one side, with 'wet paint' footprints in colors matching the cover, separating the lyrics. On the reverse were credits, along with a note stating, 'REO is still Neal Doughty, Alan Gratzer, Gary Richrath, Kevin Cronin, Bruce Hall' as if to reassure fans and the group that the group would ride out this storm. Both of Richrath's tunes were written with the Kelly and Steinberg team. A third song by the three of them, 'Desperate Lover,' ended up on Darlene Love's 1988 album *Paint Another Picture*. 'Desperate Lover' (produced by Kelly and Steinberg) has a solid groove with a bass line that almost ventures into Peter Gunn territory. The soulful, bluesy rock track features harmonica and horns, and Love's robust vocals certainly do it justice. If there's a demo of this song featuring Richrath's guitar work, it's never surfaced.

To promote the album, Epic sent to radio the double vinyl LP *Life as We Know It: World Premiere Weekend*. The first LP was an interview with Kevin Cronin; the second was the music from *Life as We Know It*. The 'Live as We Know It' tour began in February 1987 and included stops in Venezuela at the end of the year. 'A Night at the Met,' a Hollywood Palladium charity gig to benefit the homeless hosted by radio station KMET, was held on 23 February 1987. About a half dozen acts, including Ozzy Osbourne and Little Steven, performed. REO were the last to hit the stage and played 'New Way to Love,' 'One too Many Girlfriends,' 'Don't Let Him Go,' 'Variety Tonight,' and 'Roll with the Changes.' Most acts then returned to the stage to perform John Lennon's 'Give Peace a Chance.'

The show on 18 July 1987 at Kiel Auditorium in Saint Louis, Missouri, was recorded for Westwood One radio for broadcast in October. The performance of 'That Ain't Love' from that show was later issued on *Second Decade*. 'Time for Me to Fly,' from the same show, was included on *Setlist: The Very Best of REO Speedwagon Live*. Also in 1987, Canada's *Good Rockin' Tonite* featured a brief interview with Doughty, Cronin, and Richrath.

The setlist changed over the tour, but performances variously included 'New Way to Love,' 'That Ain't Love,' 'In My Dreams,' 'One Too Many Girlfriends,' 'Variety Tonight,' and 'Screams and Whispers.' During this tour, Cronin and Hall formed The Strolling Dudes. As The Dudes, the two of them would perform 'incognito' for fun during after-show parties at whatever hotel they were staying. When the tour ended, they continued getting together to play, eventually bringing in other musicians, including drummer Graham Lear and guitarist Miles Joseph, and performing at L.A. clubs.

'New Way to Love' (Cronin) (4:07)

The up-tempo opening song's message is, at first, about finding common ground in a love affair and making things work when the people involved are opposites. From the first line of, 'Maybe we don't need to share the same roof,' the singer sees all that's not working while looking at what it might take to bridge those differences. At the same time, the lyrics seem to acknowledge the differences in personalities in the band's personal and musical relationships and the willingness to work around them to keep the band alive: 'Maybe we don't need to see eye to eye.'

Hall deftly works the frets on his bass, throwing funk into the rock tune. Doughty works the piano and Lon Price, who contributed to 1978's 'Say You Love Me or Say Goodnight' partners with Greg Smith to add rowdy sax to the mix. Smith has worked with scores of artists from Kansas to Tom Petty, but this album is his only work with REO.

The instrumental break mid-song brings an excellent REO keyboard/guitar volley, Doughty hammering away on piano, Richrath breaking in with a searing guitar lead, Doughty returning with hot licks, and Richrath squeezing out a few more notes before Cronin is there with another verse. Through it all, the lyrics and musical tone remain optimistic, declaring with conviction, 'We're gonna find a *new* way to love.'

'That Ain't Love' (Cronin) (4:00)

Starting with stern acoustic strumming, 'That Ain't Love' drives straight into the heart of the listener. The first smoldering notes of electric guitar add desperation to the dispirited lyrics. Cronin has said he wrote this at a time his home life was splintering. Unlike 'New Way to Love,' the lyrics aren't looking for reconciliation. It's clear that whatever's going on isn't affection or love in any form. Cronin's vocals match the lyrics, coming across as spiteful and accusatory, more so every time the chorus comes around. The song was originally intended to be a duet with Cheap Trick's Robin Zander, hence the reference in the liner notes: 'Special Thanks To: Robin Zander (The best-laid plans).'

Doughty's synthesizer bops through the verses. Richrath's solo is short but searing, adding fuel to the anger of the song. Background vocals are credited to Tom Kelly and Bob Carlisle, billed as The Honkettes. Kelly had been working with the band for nearly ten years, but this was Carlisle's first time with REO, where he performed on four tracks. A decade later, Carlisle scored a huge hit in the US and Canada with 'Butterfly Kisses.' The synthesizer and drums have that 1980s feel. When the song made it into later tours, it was slightly rearranged, with less synthesizer and a more bluesy sound. This was the first single released from the album, climbing to 16 in the US and 82 in Canada.

'In My Dreams' (Cronin, Tom Kelly) (4:31)

Cronin has mentioned several times, including in July 2020's *Songs & Stories from Camp Cronin*, Episode 17, that 'In My Dreams' is his wife Lisa's favorite REO song. The two have performed it together many times. Cronin wrote most of the song in 1975, working in Gary Loizzo's four-track garage recording studio where they also conspired on some of Cronin's other demos, including 'Time for Me to Fly,' 'Keep Pushin',' and 'Can't Fight This Feeling.' At the time, it was more of a folk tune and Cronin had the melody, verses, and bridge but struggled with the chorus. It wasn't until *Life as We Know It* that he took 'In My Dreams' to Kelly and they completed it.

It's a gentle track about lost love. It's now only in his dreams that the singer is with the love of his life: 'I keep hopin' one day I'll awaken and somehow she'll be lying by my side.' Whether she's passed away and left him to grieve or merely ended their relationship and he's longing for reconciliation isn't clear. The acoustic guitar and soft synthesizer keep the tune light but thoughtful. A soft-edged electric guitar solo plays out over a few measures without breaking the spell. Kelly, Carlisle, and Cronin handle backing vocals, while Forman assists with percussion.

A video for the song, with band members' families featured throughout, was directed by Chicago-born Jim Yukich. Shortly before the halfway point, Cronin is seen holding up a Strolling Dudes t-shirt. And yes, that parrot appearing in a few shots did relieve itself on Cronin's shoulder. 'In My Dreams' was the third single from the album, hitting number 19 in the US and 61 in Canada. It remained on the US charts the longest of any REO single, at 30 weeks.

'One Too Many Girlfriends' (Cronin) (3:54)
There's nothing subtle about this rock track. The lyrics tell of someone who's overindulging, living too close to the edge, dating too many women at the same time. There are car metaphors ('runnin' lights for years, grindin' down those forward gears') and criticisms ('he needs a change, he needs more than a phone booth'), but in the end, it's not about girlfriends. It's a message from Cronin to Richrath about getting his life back on track.

In case the message isn't clear, Cronin sings the line, 'he's gonna take it on the run, before it runs him down,' a deliberate reference to Richrath's 'Take It on the Run.' Despite this, Richrath still dishes out hot licks, pulling off a soaring solo – maybe just to disprove Cronin's lyrics. Kelly and Carlisle help on backing vocals again.

'Variety Tonight' (Doughty) (4:22)
Side one of the original cassette and LP ends with a Doughty-penned number, 'Variety Tonight.' The track fades in on synthesizer, creating pressure as the intro slowly intensifies. Drums and bass join, adding to the moodiness. Richrath's first electric notes further the atmosphere while Hall lays down some brilliant bass, plucking away while providing the underlying rhythm. About a minute into the song, Cronin's vocals begin: 'If ever you think you miss the thrill of the chase.'

'Variety Tonight' is about keeping things fresh and lively in a relationship, specifically in the romantic sense and shaking things up in the bedroom: 'I can be different, honey, I can be new.' Richrath's blistering guitar solo adds to the smoldering attitude while the rest of the band work the groove. Background singers Terry Wood and sisters Julia Waters and Maxine Waters give the song a gospel edge. Julia and Maxine Waters have performed on hundreds of records, working on releases by everyone from Gino Vannelli to Cher. Wood's background vocals can be found again on *The Earth, a Small Man, His Dog and a Chicken*. The track ends on the singers' a cappella 'Make you feel right.' 'Variety Tonight' was released as a single and hit number 60 in the US.

'Screams and Whispers' (Richrath, Tom Kelly, Billy Steinberg) (3:27)
'Screams and Whispers' is another relationship song, this time about being brutally honest with each other. The song's narrator is begging his partner to

89

tell the truth about what she's feeling and thinking, and 'whatever we uncover, we can make it, make it alright.' The track seems to be part of the ongoing dialogue within the band as it fights to hold itself together, the lyrics as much about a romantic couple as it is about a musical partnership.

Richrath plays an inspired solo, squeezing screams and whispers out of his guitar with each squealing note. Doughty pummels the keyboards under Richrath's guitar break before taking over with his own solo on synthesizer sax. This is the first of two tracks Richrath co-wrote for the album. If Richrath was getting disheartened with the band and having trouble creating new material, he hides it well and more than makes up for it with his solos across the entire LP.

'Can't Get You Out of My Heart' (Cronin, Tom Kelly, Billy Steinberg) (3:33)
This one has a definite 1980s power pop flavor. It's an upbeat number where the singer contemplates breaking up with his girlfriend but never does because she's forever in his soul and heart.

Carlisle returns, working backing vocals with Cronin. Doughty proves a light touch on the synths, riffing under the chorus but never breaking out into a bona fide solo. Richrath has little to no presence. Hall, however, comes up with driving bass lines for the bridge as Cronin sings, 'I look at you sometimes, I see the woman I love.' Gratzer, who's been unobtrusively keeping time throughout the tune, shifts into a light gallop toward the end. The synths and drums may sound a little dated, but overall, it's a fun track.

'Over the Edge' (Richrath, Tom Kelly, Billy Steinberg) (3:57)
In retrospect, this Richrath co-write can be assumed to be part confessional, part apology, and loosely autobiographical. It gives a glimpse of what Richrath was going through at the time with lines like 'I was always out of my head' and 'I wouldn't listen to what anybody said.'

After a quick fade-in on electric guitar, the first verse begins with the protagonist telling how he's done wrong before jumping into the chorus. Drugs are part of the problem as the lyrics tell of 'cuttin' with a razor blade, spendin' every cent I made, o-o-o-o-over the edge.' The instrumental break hits, Hall's thick bass laying a foundation as Richrath plunges into it, wringing out his emotions, guitar wailing and climbing. Then Cronin's back with an odd, cheerleader-style chant for the line, 'If I had died, it would've been a shame.'

After the final chorus, it's time for more from Richrath, closing out the track with another brilliant solo. Here, he's working up and down the neck of his Gibson, hitting the whammy, ripping into fast licks, making the instrument interpret his every emotion. The song finishes with an effect that evokes falling from on high. 'Over the Edge' was the B-side to the ballad 'In My Dreams,' which would've been a stunning contrast for anyone who flipped the single over and heard it for the first time.

'Accidents Can Happen' (Hall, Jeffrey B. Hall) (4:18)

This is the second time Hall shared songwriting credits with his brother Jeffrey, after 'Thru the Window' from *Wheels are Turnin.'* As already noted, some tracks on *Life as We Know It* have a 1980s flavor, but this is the only one with definite new wave overtones. There's delicious humor here, the narrator contemplating homicide but knowing he doesn't want to end up in prison. Instead, he fantasizes about a tire flying off an automobile, using a voodoo doll, poison, electrocution, and more.

Hall handles the lead vocals, sometimes climbing into falsetto territory to keep it light-hearted as he reminds his target of all the accidents that can happen. Synth and bass push the song, and the guitar solo is short and quirky, in keeping with the new wave spirit. 'Accidents Can Happen' was the flipside to 'That ain't Love.'

'Tired of Gettin' Nowhere' (Cronin) (4:10)

Like the closer on *Wheels are Turnin,'* *Life as We Know It* finishes with a power track, jumping right into the meat of the song. The tune launches with a few measures of flirty, slightly distorted guitar and choppy synthesizer before digging into the chorus. The song is equally about being trapped in a lifeless romantic relationship and about being caught in a rock band where things are not working out. It's the opposite sentiment of the previous album's optimistic 'Wheels are Turnin',' but the performance and energy levels are a match.

Horns make the song. Price and Smith appear again, along with Cronin's son Paris, Nick Lan, Lee Thornburg, and Rick Braun. Braun was part of Hall and Cronin's Strolling Dudes side project and would co-write (with Cronin) 'Here with Me' for *The Hits*. About two minutes into the track, the rowdy horn section takes over, then Richrath answers with a short solo before the horns respond with another brief bit. Soon Doughty jumps in with organ, swiping and darting across the keys, lifting it higher. On backing vocals, Wood and the Waters sisters take another turn, helping bring 'Tired of Gettin' Nowhere' to a close as Cronin shouts, 'Get some rest!'

The Hits (1988)

Personnel:
Kevin Cronin: lead vocals, guitar
Gary Richrath: lead guitar
Neal Doughty: keyboards, synthesizers
Alan Gratzer: drums
Bruce Hall: bass guitar
Gregg Philbin: bass guitar on 'Keep Pushin',' 'Ridin' the Storm Out' (Live)
Tommy Funderburk: background vocals on 'I Don't Want to Lose You,' 'Here with Me'
Eric Persing: programming and additional synthesizers on 'I Don't Want to Lose You,' 'Here with Me'
Producers: Various, Keith Olsen on 'I Don't Want to Lose You' and 'Here with Me'
Engineers: Various
Record Label: Epic Records
Released: 18 May 1988
Running Time: 51:07 LP, 62:26 CD
Highest Chart Place: US: 56, UK: –

Similar to the statement included with *Life as We Know It*, the liner notes here state, 'REO Speedwagon is Kevin Cronin, Gary Richrath, Neal Doughty, Alan Gratzer, Bruce Hall,' to reassure fans that the classic line-up was still intact. But Gratzer and Richrath had both departed the band within a year of *The Hits* hitting the shops, dissolving the most commercially successful line-up of REO. This is the last release with new material while Richrath and Gratzer were in the band. Gratzer was already moving toward retirement, but Richrath was still intending to work on material for the next studio record.

In addition to the previously-released hits, two new tracks ('I Don't Want to Lose You,' 'Here With Me') appeared on the album. Both were produced by Keith Olsen, who had previously produced Kelly's band Fools Gold as well as acts like Sons of Champlin, Fleetwood Mac, and Pat Benatar. As was often the case in the late 1980s and early 1990s, the CD had bonus tracks that were not on the vinyl record. Epic added Doughty's Top 20 'One Lonely Night' and Hall's 'Back on the Road Again,' which was never a single but is one of the most recognized REO tracks. The cover is a simple, striking image, mostly in black and white. Large white letters are jumbled in a pile but spell out H I T S.

The Hits is an excellent collection and great starting point for anyone new to the band, though like a lot of 'greatest' retrospectives, it wasn't all-inclusive. No songs from *Good Trouble* made the cut, despite 'Keep the Fire Burnin'' hitting number 7 in the US and 'Sweet Time' climbing to 26. Upon its release, the album reached number 56 in the US and 62 in Canada. It has been certified four times platinum for selling over four million copies in the US, and earned silver certification in the UK.

92

When Gratzer announced he was retiring to spend more time with his family after being on the road for nearly 20 years, the band brought in Strolling Dudes drummer Graham Lear. He'd played on several Santana albums and worked with such artists as Gino Vannelli and Canadian group Natural Gas. Lear was already familiar with some of the REO road crew, having met them while attending hockey games in L.A. He also knew David DeVore, who worked on both *Wheels are Turnin'* and *Life as We Know It*, through their golf games.

'I got a call from David DeVore one day, and he said there's a couple of the guys from REO, they have this band called The Dudes and they're looking for a drummer.' The offer was initially to play every Wednesday night at a club called Ten Pesos in Encino, California. Lear was on a break from the road and the club wasn't far from his home, so he accepted the offer, even though he was more into jazz and fusion than what The Dudes might be playing.

The Strolling Dudes started out playing cover songs, as well as REO songs, and added originals like 'Love is a Rock,' which ended up on the next REO studio record. When REO went back on the road, the line-up was now Gratzer, Doughty, Richrath, Cronin, and Lear.

Lear has good memories of 'doing the tour with Gary,' and at some point, worked with Richrath, Hall, Doughty, Tom Deluca, and Michael Jahnz on demo songs intended for the next REO album. 'There for a couple of days, he had me play drums on some of the songs. I thought they were very good. I don't know if they ever got released.' He added, 'Shortly after that, it was announced that Gary wasn't going to do the next tour.' It's not clear if any of the music from the Lear sessions made it onto Richrath's 1992 CD with Jahnz, and Lear has lost his cassette of those demos.

When Richrath and the band parted ways in early 1989 due to creative differences, Miles Joseph from The Strolling Dudes was brought in as a replacement. Joseph had joined REO prior to shows in Puerto Rico and Chile in early 1989, but by the time the band started work on their next studio album, both Joseph and Lear had departed, replaced by Dave Amato and Bryan Hitt, respectively. Joseph, who had been in the band Player and worked with acts like Bob Dylan and Edgar Winter, passed away in December 2012. Coincidentally, Amato toured briefly with a re-formed Player in early 1988.

The Songs:

'I Don't Want to Lose You,' 'Here with Me,' 'Roll with the Changes,' 'Keep on Loving You,' 'That ain't Love,' 'Take It on the Run,' 'Don't Let Him Go,' 'Can't Fight this Feeling,' 'Keep Pushin',' 'In My Dreams,' 'Time for Me to Fly,' 'Ridin' the Storm Out' (Live), CD Bonus Tracks: 'One Lonely Night,' 'Back on the Road Again'

The New Songs
'I Don't Want to Lose You' (Tom Kelly, Billy Steinberg) (3:07)
This rock track was written by Kelly and Steinberg. Kelly had been making appearances on REO records since *Tuna Fish*, and Steinberg had co-written

songs on *Life as We Know It*. The two had been working together for several years and released one album under the band name i-TEN in 1981. In recognition of their impact on the music industry, Kelly and Steinberg were inducted into the American Songwriters Hall of Fame in 2011.

Despite the song having a late 1980s synth sound, 'I Don't Want to Lose You' has aged well. It didn't chart as a single but was firmly in the 'should've been a hit' category with its catchy chorus: '...why didn't I break down, *breeeak* down and say, I don't want to lose you.' Richrath turns in a tight solo, but he's playing a Gibson US-1 guitar instead of his Les Paul. The US-1 was also part of Richrath's arsenal on tour for *The Hits*.

One video of the song begins with Gratzer turning over duties to Lear, who then sits at the drumkit and counts in using the sticks Gratzer just handed him. It's Gratzer who performed on the record of 'I Don't Want to Lose You,' but Lear who features in the video. The video was probably most fans' first awareness that Gratzer had retired from REO. Lear remained REO's drummer for more than a year and a half and appeared on some tracks later included on *Second Decade*.

'Here with Me' (Cronin, Rick Braun) (4:53)

'Here with Me' is a ballad by Cronin and jazz trumpeter Rick Braun. Like drummer Lear, Braun was a member of the Strolling Dudes with Cronin and Hall. He also played trumpet on *Life as We Know It*'s 'Tired of Gettin' Nowhere.' In addition to his solo work of well over a dozen albums, Braun has worked in the studio or on tour with everyone from Crowded House to Tom Petty. The ballad 'Here with Me' didn't chart in the UK but reached number 20 in the US and 23 in Canada. To date, it's REO's last Top 40 hit. It's a lament about losing a love that was meant to be. Though it's over, part of that love is still 'here with me,' which provides hope that maybe what once was can be again.

Doughty's piano opens the song, setting the tone. Cronin's vocals work nicely, providing the desperate, foolishly hopeful feeling of someone who's lost the love of a lifetime. Richrath's solo is short but has teeth. Unlike 'I Don't Want to Lose You,' Gratzer performs in the video for 'Here With Me.' Tommy Funderburk provided background vocals on 'Here with Me' and 'I Don't Want to Lose You,' having also appeared on *Wheels are Turnin'* in 1984.

Related Tracks

'Everybody's Gotta Face the Music' by Kevin Cronin (Dean Pitchford, Richard Marx) (Sing soundtrack) 1989 (4:09)

The 1989 movie *Sing* (not to be confused with the 2016 animated film of the same name), a fictional story behind an annual real-life student musical production in New York City, was a box office flop but produced some memorable songs. This one was co-written by fellow Illinois musician Richard Marx.

'Everybody's Gotta Face the Music' has a *Top Gun* 'Danger Zone' feeling with a slick 1980s sound. The lyrics are uplifting and encouraging: 'There's a moment when you know you can do anything.' The same year that Cronin sang 'Everybody's Gotta Face the Music,' he supplied background vocals for 'Wait for the Sunrise' on Marx's *Repeat Offender*.

'I Don't Mind' by Jimmy Harnen and Kevin Cronin (J. Harnen, T. Owens, P.J. Williams) 1989 (3:57)
'I Don't Mind' is a twangy upbeat rock number from Jimmy Harnen's *Can't Fight the Midnight*. Harnen and Cronin trade verses, turning in a loose yet energetic performance about enjoying life wherever you are and not worrying about what you might be missing. David DeVore served as producer on the record, having already worked with Cronin on *Life as We Know It*.

The Earth, a Small Man, His Dog and a Chicken (1990)

Personnel:
Kevin Cronin: lead vocals, acoustic guitar
Neal Doughty: Hammond organ
Bruce Hall: bass guitar
Jesse Harms: keyboards, background vocals
Dave Amato: lead guitar, background vocals
Bryan Hitt: drums, percussion
Steve Forman: percussion
Producers: Ton Lord-Alge, Kevin Cronin, Jesse Harms (with Jim Scott on 'Love is a Rock,' 'The Heart Survives')
Engineer: Tom Lord-Alge
Assistant Engineers: Steve Gallagher, Mike Tacci, Julie Last (on 'Love is a Rock,' 'The Heart Survives')
Record Label: Epic Records
Release Date: 30 August 1990
Running Time: 46:05
Highest Chart Place: US: 129, UK: –

The band had risen to challenges time after time since their formation in 1967 and now came major personnel changes and the question of whether fans would support the 'new' REO. *The Earth, a Small Man, His Dog and a Chicken* had two strikes against it before it was even released. First, fans had doubts about a different line-up. Second was the timing of the album. Had this been released a decade earlier, it likely would've been a huge success. The music was pure REO and a natural successor to *Life as We Know It*, but popular music tastes (and radio playlists) had shifted.

Where *Life as We Know It*'s liner notes stated, 'REO is still…,' the notes here proclaimed, 'REO Speedwagon is now' and lists Cronin, Doughty, Hall, Harms, Amato, and Hitt. Drummer Gratzer had retired to spend more time with his family. Guitarist Richrath had departed due to creative differences. For a short while, rumors circulated there might be two REOs in the making, one under Richrath and one under Cronin, but it never happened. Richrath instead worked with Michael Jahnz (whom he'd partnered with to make demo songs for the next REO record) and Jahnz's band Vancouver and started playing live shows by late 1989. Eventually, they recorded *Only the Strong Survive*, released in 1992 under the band name Richrath.

For REO, in place of Gratzer and Richrath, first came Graham Lear and Miles Joseph, then Bryan Hitt and Dave Amato. Lear and Joseph 'and Strolling Dudes everywhere' are included under the Special Thanks note on the record. REO had been a five-piece band since the late 1960s, but that changed when Jesse Harms was added on keyboards to make it a six-piece.

Amato joined in May of 1989. He, like several other members of REO, was greatly influenced by The Beatles, and by the late 1960s, was performing in bands such as The Aftermath and Dave and the Essex. Since then, Amato has worked with everyone from Black Oak Arkansas to Motley Crue (notably singing the 'Girls, Girls, Girls' chorus), and spent three years in Ted Nugent's band, performing on *Little Miss Dangerous* and *If You Can't Lick 'em, Lick 'em*. He's also worked with Jimmy Barnes and the Elefante brothers in Mastedon (not to be confused with the metal band Mastodon) before arriving in REO. His audition for REO wasn't much more than a 30-minute jam followed by time on Cronin's basketball court, perhaps making Amato wonder if he'd got the job.

Drummer Hitt came aboard shortly after Amato, having previously played with acts like Nick Gilder, Life by Night, and Wang Chung. Hitt was the first drummer the band auditioned. Once he'd finished, the band knew they had the right man but felt an obligation to listen to the others who'd showed up.

Keyboardist Harms had worked with, among others, Sammy Hagar and Eddie Money. He was also a friend of Amato, and at one point, the two were considering putting their own band together shortly before they joined REO. Amato, in an August 2015 *Ultimate Classic Rock* article, stated it was Harms who'd recommended Amato to Cronin.

At first glance, it may have seemed odd to add a second full-fledged keyboard player to the band. It wasn't, however, without precedent. During the Murphy years in the 1970s, Murphy often played keyboards in addition to guitar. Cronin, too, sometimes played piano on REO records and in concert. Moreover, Harms was a producer and prolific songwriter. He ended up writing or co-writing six songs on the new album and served as a producer. In spite of having two full-time keyboard players onboard for this album, it has a distinct lack of piano, organ, or synthesizer showmanship, with no big solos or runs. Yet it was Harms who pushed the band back toward the REO sound rather than the Strolling Dudes sound it was starting to morph into. After the subsequent tour, Harms left REO in 1991 to get married, spend more time writing songs and teach music.

When it came time to decide on the album cover and title, the band chose a piece by surrealist Mark Ryden. Its 'Lowbrow' circus-style artwork depicted a bearded man in a top hat and suit standing behind a globe, one arm draped over it, with a chicken to one side and a small dog near the man's feet. Beneath it, a single eye. Ryden had penciled in 'the earth, a small man, his dog and a chicken' below the illustration and on a whim, the band used that line for the record's title. The inner sleeve of the vinyl record included credits, lyrics, and a photo of the six-piece band. The REO winged logo was scattered throughout. Tucked in amongst the thanks and art notes was 'Best of luck Alan and Gary.'

Although the band had plenty of talent within its ranks, four tracks here share credits with outside songwriters. At over 45 minutes, this is one of REO's longest playing records, perhaps to ensure those who took a chance on the revamped line-up got their money's worth. Or maybe the band just had plenty of music to unleash. *The Earth* stalled at number 129 in the US, REO's poorest showing in almost 15 years, and was nowhere to be found on the UK charts, though it did make its way to 38 in Switzerland. Regardless, any fan who gave the new record a chance found it to be excellent.

A show in Grand Rapids, Michigan, was recorded for another Westwood One radio show. That show's 'Live It Up' later appeared on *Second Decade*. Both 'Live It Up' and 'Can't Fight This Feeling' from Grand Rapids were included on 2010's *Setlist: The Very Best of REO Speedwagon LIVE*. The tour included stops in Puerto Rico, as well as Argentina, Ecuador, Venezuela, and Mexico. In Argentina toward the end of 1992, they performed (lip-synced) 'In My Dreams,' 'Keep on Loving You,' and 'Can't Fight this Feeling' on television program *Ritmo de la Noche* (Rhythm of the Night). It was also sometime in the early 1990s that the infamous Ventriloquist Show occurred. In Mexico, the band shared billing ('REO Speedwagon + Ventriloquist Act') and the dressing room with a ventriloquist. It may have been a low point, but the band soon bounced back to fill stadiums and amphitheaters, while still finding time in their tours for benefit performances like the November 1993 show in Hudson, Florida.

'Love is a Rock' (Cronin) (5:36)

Cronin had written 'Love is a Rock' and was performing it with The Strolling Dudes well before starting on *The Earth, a Small Man, His Dog and a Chicken*. 'Love is a Rock' was recorded in September and October 1989, five months before most of the rest of the album.

The song fades in over percussion suggestive of a rattlesnake warning, with Amato's guitar piercing through swirling keyboards. The introduction is barely 20 seconds but gives the entire album an attitude before it segues into a brief acoustic section and Cronin's vocals. Unusually for a Cronin song, it begins with the chorus. Soon the full band enters, keyboards and percussion at the fore. The lyrics are about life's uncertainties when everything is in turmoil and slipping away, but the singer's love 'is an immovable force.' The music is energetic, pointing to better days: 'Some things disappear without a chance to grow, but my love will not, my love is a rock.'

Hitt's drumming is solid and confident, punctuating the verses and choruses. Amato puts down a short, searing solo midway through, harkening back to that opening guitar salvo. Organ comes through between verses, while Hall's bass rolls along. In all, it's a fantastic introduction to the new line-up. 'Love is a Rock' made a respectable showing, climbing to 65 in the US, the last time an REO single graced *Billboard*'s Pop Singles chart.

'The Heart Survives' (Cronin, Harms) (4:50)

'The Heart Survives' is tinged with melancholy. Cronin has said in numerous interviews the track is loosely about the divorce he was going through at the time. It's a dose of self-reflection that comes too late to make a difference. In this case, the man in the failed relationship is the one mostly at fault, having refused to change his ways. The early verses are sung with a weariness and resignation deserving of the lyrics. Yet with each verse, Cronin's voice grows stronger, and the background singers bolder. After a brief, emotive guitar solo, Cronin is back, convincing himself, 'you can stand a little rain' and 'you're gonna grow again.' By then, the background singers are in gospel chorus mode, propelling the song from self-pity and regret into hope.

As with 'Love is a Rock,' 'The Heart Survives' was recorded in September and October of 1989, well before the rest of the album.

'Live It Up' (Harms) (3:58)
Harms' message here is a simple reminder that life is short. One can sit back, make excuses, and watch life go by or one can make the most of it: 'You can't hold back once you light the fuse.' It's a rowdy, up-tempo number, the band full-tilt to the end. It bounds along on keyboards while Hitt hammers away on drums. Hall keeps things steady on bass and Amato turns in a sweet but too-short solo in the mid-section. By tune's end, Amato is back, cramming in as much guitar as possible, dive bombing, working the whammy bar, and sinking his teeth into it.

'Live It Up' didn't crack the US Top 100 but did climb all the way to 6 on the Mainstream Rock chart, which tracks the most-played songs on US rock music radio. It was the final REO single to grace Canada's Hot 100 chart, making it to 81.

'All Heaven Broke Loose' (Harms, Adrian Gurvitz, Doughty) (4:11)
A play on the expression 'all hell broke loose,' meaning everything went wrong in the worst possible way, 'All Heaven Broke Loose' is the opposite. It's about love happening when it's least expected, providing salvation and sanity ('I was a little bit crazy then'). Harms and Doughty worked with outside songwriter Adrian Gurvitz on this tune. Gurvitz (The Gun, Baker Gurvitz Army) is an English guitarist who's written songs for artists like Eddie Money and co-wrote 'England, We'll Fly the Flag' for the England World Cup Squad in 1982. This is his sole work with REO.

The song exhibits a pop flavor but rocks nicely, thanks to crisp drums and guitar. For a song credited to the band's two keyboard players, the keys are present but subdued, with no organ or piano solos. Three-quarters through, Amato executes an understated solo, pulling golden tones from his guitar before turning back to the choruses. 'All Heaven Broke Loose' was the B-side of 'Live It Up.'

'Love in the Future' (Cronin, Tom Kelly) (4:31)
Kelly is back, having been part of every studio album since *Tuna Fish*. 'Love in the Future' is a lament about environmental destruction and our responsibility to the planet, wrapped in a catchy tune.

The song begins quietly in ballad mode. If rain, rivers, and air have turned toxic, 'is there love in the future for you and me?' It presents a dismal image. After two verses, the song escalates with bass, drums, and guitar. After another verse, the song swells further. The instrumental section brings blistering guitar work in sharp contrast to the song's beginning. Amato is back after the final verse and chorus, burning away wildly on guitar, carrying the song to the end, making the listener wish the music would last another minute or two.

'Half Way' (Cronin, Harms, Mark Spiro) (4:16)

Cronin and Harms collaborated with Mark Spiro for this number. Spiro has worked with everyone from John Waite to Julian Lennon and his songwriting credits include Cheap Trick's 'Mighty Wings' and Kansas' 'One Man, One Heart.'

The opening line is a clever bit, asking, 'How did we end up ending up this way?' 'Half Way' tells of a couple trying to make their relationship last, though it doesn't seem to be a true partnership. He's willing to 'walk all night' and 'stand in the pouring rain,' but needs her to work on their relationship, too, and meet him halfway. Even so, he'll do what's needed to hang on to her. The quiet verses set the tone for this ballad, while choruses are meaty and big, with backup singers, drums, and bass. Everything's bigger by the end of the song.

'Love to Hate' (Harms) (4:08)

Hitt ignites the track with cymbal and drums, followed by fiery guitar. Bass and keyboards join the fray, the keyboards slightly more prominent than in other songs on the album. The lyrics project on two levels. One is about helping each other out and providing a hand when needed, rather than bullying someone who's already down. But it's also about critics who 'tear down what you create' and take great pleasure in doing so.

Amato ducks in and out with stinging guitar between and within the verses, playing with a vengeance to match the posture of the words. At last, we get an organ solo, albeit brief, a rapid-fire blast on the keyboards to punctuate the song's defiant attitude. The track is a statement of spirited scorn toward critics and naysayers, an unapologetic 'kiss my arse' proclamation.

'You Won't See Me' (Cronin) (3:20)

Another propulsive rock track, 'You Won't See Me,' is about accepting the good and the bad in someone, rather than rejecting someone outright because 'you won't see me as I am.' Amato's guitar announces the song, winding up and inviting in the rest of the band. It's a bold number. The keyboards are somewhat more prominent, organ bumping along but never breaking into a true solo. Hitt is tireless on drums, propelling the tune and keeping it aggressive. Amato unleashes more great guitar and Cronin's vocals are strong.

Similar in sentiment to 'Love to Hate,' the attitude here is 'take me as I am or get out of my way.' To emphasize that point, as the last notes fade, a door slams shut with an echo, underscoring the lyrics, 'I'll be moving on, I'll be long gone.'

'Can't Lie to My Heart' (Cronin, Diane Warren) (4:40)
After the rock of 'You Won't See Me,' the album ventures back into power ballad territory with 'Can't Lie to My Heart,' which Cronin wrote with Diane Warren. Warren, inducted into the Songwriters Hall of Fame in 2001, is an unequivocal powerhouse who's penned hits for Cher, Cheap Trick, Chicago, and countless others.

This is a beautiful tune with gritty guitar to toughen it up. The lyrics tell of trying to deny love, 'telling myself I don't need you,' when reality is the opposite. The song takes flight from the start and the background vocals take it even higher. 'Can't Lie to My Heart' could've/should've been a hit but was never released as a single.

'L.I.A.R.' (Amato, Doughty, Hitt, Hall, Cronin) (3:08)
The song's title stands for Love Is All Right. Presumably, calling it 'Love Is All Right' would've created confusion with opening track 'Love is a Rock.' But a title that spells out 'liar' also provides a nice argument against the lyrics proclaiming how wonderful love is. The song originated with Doughty, who brought it to the band. Everyone worked on it, though the songwriting credits on the LP centre circular label omit Harms, while the sleeve notes list the credit as 'R.E.O. Speedwagon.'

A cappella vocals (with echo and other effects) start the tune, proclaiming, 'Love is all right, love is all right, whoa-ohhh, love is all right' before Amato lashes out with a few hot riffs. It's an up-tempo rocker, with Hitt never resting behind the drumkit. Cronin brings a defiant attitude with his singing, nearly spitting out the lyrics. The keyboards and bass remain mostly in the background, but the instrumental break brings more snarling guitar that matches Cronin's combative vocal style.

'Go for Broke' (Harms, Cronin, Amato, Hall) (3:26)
The album closes with this high-octane rocker, written for the Tom Cruise racing film *Days of Thunder*. Unfortunately, 'Go for Broke' never made it into the film or onto the soundtrack. Similar to 'L.I.A.R.,' the vinyl record's center label credits some band members (Harms, Cronin, Amato, and Hall) as the songwriters, while the sleeve notes credit 'R.E.O. Speedwagon.'

The track is out of the gate with Amato's guitar revving like a race car engine, shifting through gears. Cronin jumps in with, 'My life is runnin' like a stock car race, high speed and lots of curves.' The words are equally about loving and racing hard, urging no restraint in either. The lyrics in the liner notes state, 'every night I'm on the line, livin' like my days are numbered,' but

Cronin seems to be singing, 'every night I'm on the line, livin' in days of thunder.' Either way, Amato immediately jumps in with more fast-burning licks, tearing up his guitar. After the final chorus and the song winds down, Amato dives back in to rev his guitar a few more times to end the disc on an adrenaline high. 'Go for Broke' was the flipside of 'Love is a Rock.'

Related Tracks

'Hard to Believe' by Kevin Cronin and Friends (Cronin) (4:55) (1991)
Following Iraq's invasion of Kuwait in 1990 and the subsequent Persian Gulf War, Cronin wrote 'Hard to Believe.' He enlisted Bill Champlin, David Crosby (Cronin's neighbor at the time), and Richard Marx to record with him. Crosby had been in a motorcycle accident shortly before and arrived at the recording session still on crutches. The track begins in a funky mode, with Cronin and friends' gritty vocals working the chorus: 'It's hard to believe the bombs are flying, hard to believe we've stopped trying to work it out.' The singers take turns on the verses, with Cronin first, then Champlin. After the next chorus, it continues to rotate among the singers.

The Second Decade of Rock and Roll 1981 to 1991 (1991)

Personnel:
Neal Doughty: keyboards
Alan Gratzer: drums
Gary Richrath: lead guitar
Kevin Cronin: vocals, rhythm guitar
Bruce Hall: bass
Graham Lear: drums
Dave Amato: lead guitar
Bryan Hitt: drums
Carla Day, Melanie Jackson: background vocals
Record Label: Epic Records
Released: 24 September 1991
Running Time: 76:40
Highest Chart Place: US 108, UK: –

REO's second retrospective collection, following 1980's *Decade*, chronicles significant changes within the band. Out of 17 tracks, six are studio versions familiar to fans, with the remaining recordings culled from five performances in Illinois, Missouri, Hawaii, and Michigan. Although the title states *1981 to 1991*, the earliest recordings are from 1983 and include 1978's 'Roll with the Changes' from a 1983 show in Rockford, Illinois, and 1979's 'Back on the Road Again' from Honolulu, Hawaii, recorded in 1989. And technically, *Hi Infidelity* was released at the end of 1980, though it hit big in 1981.

Despite all the live tracks, it's not a live album the way 1977's *Live* was. Nor is it quite the retrospective the way the first *Decade* was because it doesn't contain enough studio tracks and doesn't present the music in chronological order. *Second Decade* falls somewhere between those two records but deserves a place in any fan's collection. This contains one of the few inclusions of anything from *Good Trouble* on a compilation. 'Keep the Fire Burnin'' is from a show in 1983, and after that tour, it was rarely played live. The album also provides a couple souvenirs of what's claimed to be Richrath's last performance as a member of REO, from a show in Honolulu, Hawaii, in early 1989. However, that appears to be an error. The Hawaii concert was actually on 19 December 1988, while Richrath's last full performance with REO was likely the 31 December 1988 show in Chicago. Regardless, those concerts were never intended to be his last with the band, but circumstances changed the following year. There was certainly nothing in his performance on these recordings to indicate any internal issues or the changes to come. His playing proved as passionate as ever.

Two tracks feature drummer Graham Lear's only officially released performances with the band: 'Back on the Road Again' and 'Keep on Loving

You '89 (Reggae Version).' The reggae 'Keep on Loving You' was a holdover from The Strolling Dudes shows. Coincidentally, these two tracks are taken from the Hawaii show that's listed as Richrath's final performance. Not long after, Lear, like Gratzer before him, departed the band to spend more time at home with his family. 'My only regret,' said Lear, 'is that I wish I could've actually recorded a whole record with them (REO). That would've been nice. It didn't happen, timing-wise.'

The final song on *Second Decade* is from Michigan in 1990. 'Live It Up' was the first official live offering from the then-new line-up featuring Amato, Hitt, and Harms. Keyboardist Harms would leave the band shortly after to focus on songwriting and music teaching, but Amato and Hitt are still with REO more than 30 years later.

Promotion efforts included a 3 October 1991 show at the Whisky a Go Go in Los Angeles, California, hosted by Jim Ladd from radio station KLSX. It was broadcast via satellite on his monthly *Sunday Night Live* program. The show included live music, cuts from *Second Decade*, and interviews with Doughty and Cronin. It was also a chance to introduce Amato and Hitt, though they'd been with the band for over a year by then. A different line-up of REO had last played the Whisky a Go Go in 1971. By some twist of fate, *Second Decade* didn't chart when it was first released. It wasn't until nearly two decades later that it finally made the US charts, entering at the magical number 157 on 19 February 2011. It eventually made it to number 13 on the Catalogue chart, and 108 on the *Billboard* 200. Not only did it chart late, but it also wasn't until 25 years later, in 2016, that it was certified gold in the US. It was the last REO album to make the *Billboard* 200.

The Songs:
'Don't Let Him Go' (Live), 'Tough Guys' (Live), 'Take It on the Run' (Live), 'Keep the Fire Burnin'' (Live), 'Roll with the Changes' (Live), 'I Do' Wanna Know' (Live), 'Can't Fight this Feeling' (Live), 'Live Every Moment,' 'That Ain't Love' (Live), 'One Too Many Girlfriends,' 'Variety Tonight,' 'Back on the Road Again' (Live), 'Keep on Loving You '89' (Reggae Version) (Live), 'Love is a Rock,' 'All Heaven Broke Loose,' 'L.I.A.R.,' 'Live It Up' (Live)

Building the Bridge (1996)

Personnel:
Kevin Cronin: lead vocals, acoustic and electric rhythm guitar, backing vocals
Neal Doughty: keyboards
Dave Amato: lead guitar, harmony vocals, rhythm and slide guitar, backing vocals
Bruce Hall: bass guitar, backing vocals, lead vocals on 'Hey, Wait a Minute'
Bryan Hitt: drums and percussion
Stephen Croe: synclavier
Producers: Greg Ladanyi, Kevin Cronin
Producer ('Then I Met You'): Stephen Croes
Engineers: Greg Ladanyi, Brett Swain
Second Engineers: Paris X. Cronin, Jeff Shannon, Geoff Spenser
Mastering: Doug Sax, Gavin Lurssen, Ron Lewter
2022 Remastering Engineer: Eric Boulanger
Record Label: Essential Records (division of Castle)
Record Label: Castle Music
Record Label: Universal International
Released: 9 July 1996
Record Label: Mailboat Records (Reissue)
Reissue Released: 27 May 2022
Running Time: 48:51
Highest Chart Place: US: –, UK: –

Six years after their last studio album, REO released *Building the Bridge*. Its main flaw? REO were no longer on Epic and their new label went bankrupt. As a result, the CD lacked promotion. Its timing also hurt, with classic rock having been shunted aside for much of the early 1990s. The songs on *Building the Bridge* were solid, the playing was great, but no one had a chance to hear it. Anyone hoping to buy the new music had to put in serious effort to find it. As a result, it was the first REO album since *R.E.O./T.W.O.* that failed to crack the *Billboard* charts and the CD was soon out of print, a situation that lasted more than 20 years. In the meantime, two songs here appeared on 1999's *The Ballads*, giving fans who missed the original release a second chance to hear them, and one of those two songs surfaced again on *The Essential REO Speedwagon*. Another track was reworked and recorded with Styx in 2009.

As the original CD liner note stated, 'The Bridge was six years in the making. It is a Bridge between the old REO and the new REO. It has connected us to an amazing group of friends, family and co-workers who have supported us through the project. And, it has connected us with you. So, let's party!' The original packaging was a low-budget affair, which may have sent the wrong message to consumers who wondered if REO had lost their shine. Early pressings of the CD booklet on Essential Records even misspelled the word 'connected' in the second to last sentence of the liner note, stating, 'it has conected (sic) us with you.' Despite its packaging shortcomings, the back cover has a great photo of the band, credited to Breeze Munson. Greg Ladanyi produced the album with Cronin. Ladanyi had previously handled production duties on records by Don Henley, Kansas, and Fleetwood Mac, among others. Even with those strong credentials, some of *Building the Bridge* feels a little overproduced at moments, though never to the point of distraction.

Despite low sales for new music, live classic rock was on the cusp of a renaissance. Tours started getting bigger and ticket sales stronger. REO toured in 1994 variously with the likes of Survivor, Cheap Trick, and Eddie Money. 1995 saw them on a bill with Fleetwood Mac and Pat Benatar. In 1996 the tour found them at different stops with Eddie Money, Blue Öyster Cult, and others. The 'Can't Stop Rockin' '96' tour included Peter Frampton and Foreigner. 1997's 'Our Time is Gonna Come' tour setlist often included 'Building the Bridge.' Of note, guitarist Richrath joined the band for its encore of '157 Riverside Avenue' at the LA County Fair show in September 1998.

Other ventures were keeping the band members busy as well. Amato lent his guitar skills to Peter Beckett's 'How Can the Girl Refuse' from the 1991 *Beckett* album. In 1994, Hitt played on Stan Bush's *Dial 818-888-8634*. That same year, Cronin and his wife, Lisa, were part of an all-star Los Angeles choir on Mark Williamson's 'Prayer for the Children' on his *Time Slipping By*. Amato also performed on John Elefante's 1995 *Windows of Heaven*. In 1998, Amato appeared on Richie Sambora's 'If God was a Woman' from *Undiscovered Soul*. 1998 saw Cronin singing backing vocals on Tommy Shaw's 'Straight Down the Line' from *7 Deadly Zens*. Cronin was also on stage at the Music for Life Concert in November 1998, honouring Richard Marx's musician father, Dick. Cronin performed 'Roll with the Changes' and assisted with Marx's 'Right Here Waiting.'

Building the Bridge was reissued on CD in May 2022, and finally available for downloading. Previously it was the only REO studio album not found on any digital music services, aside from the few tracks included on hits packages. Eric Boulanger from The Bakery served as engineer for the rerelease. Boulanger was a natural choice to work the reissue, not only for his considerable skills as a musician and engineer, but also because he'd worked with the late Doug Sax, who was part of the team for the original mastering on *Building the Bridge*. The reissue included new artwork but did not have any bonus tracks. It did, however, have a new booklet with lyrics and more comprehensive album credits than on the original 1996 set, more worthy of the music than the initial release. The reissued CD, on Jimmy Buffett's Mailboat Records label, was available for sale at regular outlets and at the REO Speedwagon / Styx / Loverboy 2022 'Live and UnZoomed' tour. Proceeds from those sales were donated to Rock to the Rescue. In January 2023, *Building the Bridge* was issued on vinyl for the first time; the music spread across two LPs.

'Can't Stop Rockin'' (Cronin, Amato, Hall) (3:51)
The first track charges in with Amato's guitar firing away over Hitt's sharp drum work and Hall's bass, as Cronin goes straight into the chorus and declares, 'I can't stop, can't stop rockin'.' The song starts fast and hard and never lets up. In case it isn't clear, even though the band is never mentioned by name, the song is about how The Beatles' ('those four boys from England') appearance on the *Ed Sullivan Show* in America in 1964 set an entire generation, specifically the members of REO, on a quest to be in a rock and roll band. Such was their influence that the first LP Cronin ever bought was *Rubber Soul*.

The lyrics tell of struggles trying to make it in music and life in general. Even when feeling like outcasts, it's the music and the rock and roll dream that keep everyone going. Midway through, Doughty can't be restrained as he rips into some honky-tonk piano. Amato follows with more smoldering guitar, searing through to the next chorus. Cronin writes in the 2022 liner notes, 'The bass and drums are a freaking freight train,' and he's right. This song alone is worth the price of the CD.

'I Still Love You' (Cronin, Stephen Stills) (4:11)
'I Still Love You,' a co-write by Cronin and Stephen Stills, first appeared on Crosby Stills & Nash's 1990 *Live It Up* as 'Haven't We Lost Enough?' When REO worked the track for *Building the Bridge*, producer Ladayni suggested the title change to 'I Still Love You,' which Cronin soon regretted. For the 2022 reissue, the title's been changed to 'Haven't We Lost Enough (I Still Love You).'

There's a bluesy country feeling to the tune. Lyrics reflect the pain and regret of divorce, which both Cronin and Stills were going through at the time. Cronin laments the loss but sings, 'Maybe someday I'll understand.' Harmony vocals on the choruses are handled by Amato, Cronin, and Hall. Lonesome-sounding slide guitar from Amato, coupled with Cronin's acoustic, adds to the melancholy mood. An electric solo tugs at the listener with each note. Amato's playing somehow manages to convey sadness and comfort at the same time. Drums and guitar carry the song through the fadeout.

'Building the Bridge' (Cronin) (4:44)
Cronin has introduced this song in concert many times by explaining he wrote it for his son, Paris, who also served as a second engineer on *Building the Bridge*. Fittingly, the lyrics begin with 'Father to son.' There's a simple message about forging connections, creating understanding, and learning forgiveness. US President Bill Clinton used the song in his reelection campaign in 1996, with his theme of 'Building a Bridge to the 21st Century.' As part of that campaign, Cronin performed the song on Daley Plaza in Chicago, the same location where an early iteration of REO played at the Moratorium on War rally in 1970.

The sometimes gospel-tinged tune maintains a steady tempo, patiently working to get its message across. The guitar solo eases in, adding texture but never overshadowing the message. When Cronin and his wife Lisa visited Israel on holiday in 2019, he played it on a rooftop in The Old City. After coordination, Cronin performed it again on the roof at the Palestinian Bethlehem Museum, symbolically building a bridge with his two very personal performances. 'Building the Bridge' was included on *The Ballads*, in a shorter 4:15 version. The song returned to REO's setlist in 2017 and has made occasional appearances since then.

'When I Get Home' (Cronin) (4:33)

'When I Get Home' made it into the setlist on the 1995 tour while REO were still working on the forthcoming album. It begins with acoustic guitar, building quickly as organ and drums tumble in to create an early Beatles feel.

It's about being away on the road and anticipating the reunion that will follow upon returning home. Cronin has introduced the song saying he and his wife try not to be apart for more than ten days when he's touring. That isn't always possible, however, and the song was inspired while he was missing his wife but anticipating 'the first thing we're gonna do when I get home.' Doughty's organ sails along smoothly while Amato handles guitar with a light touch but gives it enough snarl to put grit into the tune. The backing vocals, combined with Hitt's drumming, provide an exciting sense of anticipation.

'Then I Met You' (Cronin) (4:52)

There's a sentiment in this love song that may be overlooked by the casual listener. Cronin sings how everything changed when he met the love of his life, but questions how he wrote his early love songs when he only *thought* he was in love. 'I've heard my songs over the radio,' he sings, and adds, 'I would listen to my own words and wonder why they'd never ring true.' It's almost a confession that he didn't mean what he said the first time around.

Nevertheless, there's a gentle swaying conjured through piano, Synclavier, and guitar, creating a beautiful, heartfelt song. The background vocals are unlike anything on the rest of the album, softly 'ooh-ooh'-ing in typical harmony in the chorus but then moving slightly deeper in a chant for the 'I never thought' verse and again toward the song's ending, adding intrigue. Stephen Croes, who also produced this tune, handles the Synclavier orchestration and performance.

'Look the Other Way' (Cronin) (3:28)

'Look the Other Way' is a raucous, up-tempo rocker about doing one's best to ignore the reality of a partner's infidelity, the musical tone conflicting with the subject matter. 'I know she's sleeping with him, but it can't be true,' sings Cronin in the role of a man standing by as his girlfriend cheats on him. Even when declaring 'this game must end,' he's still in denial.

After a couple of spirited verses, the bridge brings acoustic guitar to the front while the lyrics ponder forgiveness: 'Wouldn't I be the one that you'd come running to?' Soon it's back to rocker mode and a return to the first verses. The instrumental section allows Amato to blast hot licks over the pounding drums and bass. Hitt sounds like he's having a good time, pushing 'Look the Other Way' solidly forward without taking over. The song begins to fade out, then Hitt returns and punctuates the ending with one last bash on the drum kit.

'After Tonight' (Hall) (4:44)
The harder-edged 'Look the Other Way' is followed by 'After Tonight,' an acoustic ballad Hall wrote in 1994. From the start, he wanted Cronin to sing it. Cronin, on the other hand, wanted Hall to handle vocals. Hall's insistence on Cronin singing won in the end. It's a poignant, touching track, with Amato, Cronin, and Hall all on acoustic guitars. Croes is back on Synclavier and handles the string arrangement. Luis Conte, who also helped on 'Building the Bridge,' returns to assist with percussion.

A sadness permeates 'After Tonight,' Cronin softly singing about taking love for granted and letting it slip away, promising to be a better man. Instead of a powerful electric guitar solo, there's gentle acoustic picking to reinforce the loneliness and pain of what was lost. A shorter version (4:09) of 'After Tonight' surfaced on 1999's *The Ballads*.

'Hey Wait a Minute' (Hall) (5:20)
On the 1996 release, the song title had no comma, something the reissue corrected in the name of grammar ('Hey, Wait a Minute'). Hall handles lead vocals, something fans look forward to on every REO release. It's a treasure, a quirky, flat-out fun tune with New Orleans horns and a laid-back, funky vibe about life not turning out as expected. The small but mighty horn section consists of trumpeter Jerry Hey (who's worked with everyone from Michael Jackson to Dan Fogelberg), Lew McCreary (Steely Dan, Frank Zappa) on trombone, and Daniel L. Higgins (Aerosmith, Kenny Loggins) on saxophone. Hitt's drumming and Hall's bass set the groove as Hall daydreams and declares, 'I'm supposed to be dining on caviar and drinking Dom Perignon.' Doughty delivers an organ solo in the middle section, with Amato later laying down smooth guitar while the background singers 'shoo-shoo' away.

'One True Man' (Cronin) (4:43)
'One True Man' is a return to ballad territory. It's a true love song, a declaration about being a better person and promising 'in front of the world to be your one true man.' There's sincerity without overdoing it.

The song would fit in well on country radio, acoustic guitars providing an uncomplicated, simple feeling. Croes returns on Synclavier. The choruses are big, with drums and sweeping organ. Amato's guitar break opens up the song and ensures the 'power' in the ballad.

'She's Gonna Love Me' (Cronin, Amato) (4:01)

This is Amato's second co-write on the album, which shifts from ballad back
to rocker. It starts with studio chatter and a 'one, two, one, two, three' count-
in on Hitt's drumsticks. Then it's electric guitar and cymbals and someone
yells out, 'Wooo!' to launch the song.

Here, the singer gloats, telling a former, ungrateful girlfriend how she's lost
out on everything he has to offer, and letting her know he was the best she'll
ever have. She took him for granted and now he has a new girlfriend and
'she's gonna love me like you never could.' Amato tears it up, wailing and
burning through the lively track. After all that, it winds down with a few last
piano and guitar notes into a round of light applause in the studio. The whole
song has an energetic, early-take feel.

'Ballad of the Illinois Opry' (Cronin) (4:10)

There's an autobiographical tale here, similar to 'Music Man.' As a teenager
visiting one of Abraham Lincoln's early homes in Springfield, Illinois, Cronin
came across an outdoor pavilion called the Illinois Opry about 25 miles
outside of town. That chance encounter was the catalyst for this song, which
he states in the CD's liner notes that he wrote in 1969 as a 17-year-old.

The guitars have a country twang, fitting for an 'opry' song. Cronin opens
his heart, telling of his hopes and dreams as that teenager that day, yearning
to be a star. He promises, 'I'm gonna be up on that stage someday.' The
Illinois Opry closed around 1978, so Cronin never did get to perform on its
stage, but the dream never left him and has taken him on a 50-plus-year
journey, playing on thousands of other stages across the globe.

Many of the verses do sound more like a 17-year-old's journal entry than
the professional lyrics that flowed later, but that adds to the charm: 'Now I
don't want you people to think that all there is around Springfield, Illinois,
are landmarks telling 'bout the good old Lincoln years.' 'Ballad of the Illinois
Opry' originally had as many as ten verses and many repeat choruses.
Producer Ladanyi worked with Cronin to distill it to just over four minutes.
It's a fascinating glimpse into what Cronin dreamed of back then, and how he
kept pushing to make the dream come true.

Related Tracks

'Into the Light' (Cronin) (1993) [Unreleased]

In the early 1990s, rumors circulated that Cronin was working on a solo
album, but it never materialized. He did, however, introduce new music
around that time. One of the new tunes was 'Into the Light,' heard on a radio
broadcast in St. Louis in 1993. The song is probably similar to what Cronin
was performing as a solo folk artist in the early 1970s. It's Cronin on acoustic
guitar, accompanied by piano.

It's about the frustration of 'trying to live up to those I admire' and the
'endless roads' of trying to be someone else, instead of looking inward for

direction. He sings, 'day by day, I will find my own way, in my own fashion.' There's a sentiment that's revisited on some of 2007's *Find Your Own Way Home*, about a time to forgive, about regrets over things said, and summoning the strength to move forward.

'Cry Alone' (Cronin) (1993) [Unreleased]
'Cry Alone' is another acoustic tune Cronin performed on the 1993 radio broadcast. This time he's accompanied by congas and piano. The song is about looking at those who seem to have everything in life, including true love, but then discovering it's simply an illusion and a deliberate one at that. It's 'just another lesson to be learned.'

'Can't Stop Rockin'' with Styx (Cronin, Tommy Shaw) (4:34) (2009)
In 2009, Styx and REO convened at Vannelli's Blue Moon Studio to record a new version of 'Can't Stop Rockin'' in support of their pending joint tour of the same name. This recording, aside from the chorus, consists of entirely new lyrics. The track is now about persevering through difficult times and letting loose when the chance comes around.

The sleeve notes list all members of REO and Styx (Tommy Shaw, James 'JY' Young, Ricky Phillips, Lawrence Gowan, Todd Sucherman, Chuck Panozzo) as performing on the track. Shaw and Cronin alternate lead vocals, exchanging verses, both bands joining on the chorus. As expected, there's explosive musicianship befitting the tune's title. Guitars are at turns sharp, gritty, and sweet. Drums, bass, and keyboards fill out the song without turning things muddy or drowning out each other. It was co-produced and co-engineered by REO associate Vannelli and long-time Styx engineer, producer, front-of-house engineer and live sound mixer (over 1,500 shows) Gary Loizzo.

The 2009 'Can't Stop Rockin'' CD single, housed in a 12" by 12" sleeve like a vinyl LP, also featured 'Blue Collar Man' (live) and 'Roll with the Changes' (live) from the 2000 *Arch Allies* CD. The single was sold at live shows and on the bands' websites. It was later featured on *Rock Band 4*.

The Ballads (1999)
Personnel:
Kevin Cronin: vocals, rhythm guitar
Neal Doughty: keyboards
Alan Gratzer: drums
Gary Richrath: guitar
Bruce Hall: bass guitar
Dave Amato: guitar
Bryan Hitt: drums
Jess Harms: keyboards
Producers: various, Peter Asher on 'Just for You'
Engineers: various, Noel Golden on 'Just for You,' Eddie Delana on 'Till the Rivers Run Dry'
Record label: Epic Records
Released 3 August 1999 in US, 17 January 2000 in UK
Running Time: 55:24
Highest Chart Position: US: –, UK: –

The Ballads, like *The Hits*, is a compilation of previously released favorite songs with two newly recorded tracks to sweeten the offering for fans who may already have everything else in their collections. Over half of the album spotlights the Richrath/Gratzer line-up, but five songs feature the Amato/Hitt line-up. While all the songs on the album are appropriate for the ballad theme, seven of the 13 tracks had already appeared on *The Hits*. Nothing from *Good Trouble* made the cut. 'Sweet Time' reached number 26 in the US and would've worked well in place of one of the many repeats from *The Hits*.

Although this was an Epic release, it included the title track and 'After Tonight' from *Building the Bridge*, the first record in the history of REO that was not on Epic. Since *Building the Bridge* was so difficult to find after its initial release, this was many fans' only chance to hear those two tracks until *Building the Bridge* was reissued in 2022. It's unfortunate *The Ballads* did not chart in the US or elsewhere because the new songs deserved a much wider audience.

The Songs:
'Just for You,' 'Time for Me to Fly,' 'Keep on Loving You,' 'Can't Fight this Feeling', 'Take It on the Run,' 'Till the Rivers Run Dry,' 'In My Dreams,' 'Here with Me,' 'Building the Bridge,' 'One Lonely Night,' 'The Heart Survives,' 'After Tonight,' 'I Wish You Were There'

The New Songs
'Just for You' (Cronin, Jim Peterik) (4:38)
A piano-based love song, this is one of several that Cronin has written with Grammy Award winner Jim Peterik. The two met when Peterik was in Ides of

March ('Vehicle') and before Cronin was in REO. As Peterik tells it in his *Through the Eye of the Tiger* memoir, Cronin even booked Ides of March to appear at a dance at Cronin's high school.

Peterik has also been part of Survivor ('Eye of the Tiger'), has been a successful solo artist, and had a hand in writing classic songs for .38 Special, Cheap Trick, Sammy Hagar, Dennis DeYoung, and others. Peter Asher, from Peter and Gordon and forever associated with The Beatles, produced 'Just for You.' David Campbell, who has worked with hundreds of musicians, including Paul McCartney, Metallica, and Adele, handled the string arrangement.

When Peterik and Cronin sat down to write the song, Peterik started trying various chords on piano and soon the two had 'Just for You.' Appropriately, the song begins on piano, with Cronin almost tiptoeing in for the first verse. Hitt's drums and the string arrangement accentuate the big choruses. After the second chorus, Amato lays down a short, moving guitar solo. Cronin sings, 'And I believe in forever, just for you and me.' It finishes on piano, as it began.

'Till the Rivers Run Dry' (Cronin, Jimmy Scott) (4:15)
Cronin produced 'Till the Rivers Run Dry,' a co-write with Jimmy Scott. Scott is also a producer and a prolific songwriter whose work has been recorded by artists like Chicago and Cheap Trick. 'It was an idea that I brought to Kevin Cronin,' said Scott. 'It was quite well developed already and he liked it and put his own stamp and the REO Speedwagon vibe to it.' It was Scott's first time working with Cronin: 'He was very gracious and a delight to work with.'

This is a beautiful guitar-based song, with a country music undercurrent, about love that endures: 'Til all the rivers run dry, I'll be loving you.' Subtle harmony vocals add softness and sincerity to the lyrics.

Related Tracks
'Don't Tell Me' by Majic Ship (1999) (Amato, Mike Garrigan) (4:06)
About the time *The Ballads* was being compiled, several members of REO were working on rock tunes in a side project around the resurrected Majic Ship, with original Ship members Mike Garrigan and Tommy Nikosey. Majic Ship released an album of psychedelic rock in 1969 before disbanding after most of their instruments were lost in a house fire. Amato met Garrigan a couple decades later while both were working with Cher on her *Heart of Stone* tour. Eventually, the two collaborated on Majic Ship's *Songwaves Project* (coproduced and co-engineered by Amato), which also featured Hall and Doughty.

In 'Don't Tell Me,' the lyrics tell of a man still in love with a woman who no longer loves him back: 'Don't tell me that you love me, 'cause that's not true. What can I do, 'cause I still love you.' The track begins with Amato cranking out a loose, funky, hand jive beat. Bass, drums, and organ join in before Garrigan starts the first verse. Amato plays some seriously fun guitar between the verses before turning in a smoldering solo halfway through.

'Don't Tell Me' is definitely worth finding for any fan who wants to hear more of Amato's guitar work.

'Shameless' (Billy Joel) by Dave Amato (1999) (4:29)

This one's from the charity album *A Tribute to Garth Brooks (New Friends in Low Places)* in the US and *Hats Off to Garth Brooks* in the UK. Billy Joel wrote it, but it was Garth Brooks who turned it into a country hit. Here, Amato proves to be as adept playing and singing country music as he is performing rock. It's another chance to hear how versatile and talented the guitarist is, even outside REO. The *Tribute* album has been repackaged multiple times under multiple titles, but the music is the same on all issues.

'Between Two Fires' (Cronin, Jim Peterik) by Jim Peterik and World Stage (2000) (4:37)

In the late 1990s, Peterik started formulating plans for a revolving group of super musicians he'd worked with over his career. When it crystalized, it was known as Jim Peterik and World Stage. Peterik and his band, working with guest artists, released a CD shortly before performing their first show in January 2000.

Among the guest artists on the CD and at the debut concert was Cronin. 'Between Two Fires' is a duet, with Peterik and Cronin turning in strong vocal performances as they alternate verses. The power ballad, featuring a mandolin, is about temptation and being 'stranded at a fork in the road of love and desire.' A live version, also featuring Cronin, was released on the 2002 Jim Peterik and World Stage *Rock America* album.

'Just for You' (Cronin, Jim Peterik) by Jim Peterik & World Stage (2019) (4:54)

Peterik released another World Stage studio record, titled *Winds of Change*, in 2019, and included a recording of 'Just for You.' Surprisingly, it's not a duet, but features Cronin on lead vocals for the entire song. As it happens, it was the original recording of the song Peterik and Cronin wrote, which REO then used as a guide when crafting their own recording. The song doesn't stray much from the REO version on *The Ballads*, though keyboards are slightly more prominent and some lyrics are rearranged. It's a treat to hear Peterik playing on the tune.

Arch Allies: Live at Riverport (2000)

Personnel:
Kevin Cronin: lead vocals, rhythm guitar, vocals
Neal Doughty: keyboards
Dave Amato: lead guitar, backing vocals
Bruce Hall: bass, backing vocals, lead vocals on 'Back on the Road Again'
Bryan Hitt: drums
Executive Producer: Tom Consolo
Producers: Joe Vannelli, Cronin
Co-producer: Amato
Label: CMC International Records, Sanctuary Records
Recorded: 9 June 2000
Released: 26 September 2000
Running Time (REO Disc Only): 62:08
Highest Chart Place: US: –, UK: –

REO and Styx had been friendly rivals from the start but had never toured together until 2000, though they did share a bill as far back as 6 January 1975 in Owensboro, Kentucky (during the REO Murphy/Philbin years). The 2000 outing was christened the 'Arch Allies' tour. On the road, since both were headliner acts, they alternated the closing slot. Of note on this outing, near the start of the tour in May at a show in Los Angeles, Richrath joined REO during their encore. *Arch Allies: Live at Riverport* is a memento of the 2000-2001 tour, a two-disc set with one disc devoted to Styx and one to REO. Both discs feature the same encores where the bands jammed together on one Styx and one REO classic. A DVD was released about six weeks after the CD. As expected, the record focuses on the hits, but it's somewhat disappointing that the band couldn't squeeze in anything from the Amato/Hitt studio albums.

The 'Arch Allies' in the title has a two-fold meaning. First, both Styx and REO originated in Illinois and have been playing the same circuits for decades. Because of that, they were sometimes assumed to be arch-rivals in competition with each other. To hit the road together, striving to best each other night after night, was an interesting concept, a touring battle of the bands. Second, the show that comprised *Arch Allies* was recorded at Riverport Amphitheater on the outskirts of Saint Louis. One of the most recognized landmarks in the US is the 630-foot (over 190 meters) stainless steel Gateway Arch on the west bank of the Mississippi river in Saint Louis. The Arch, built in the early 1960s and stylized on the *Arch Allies* cover, is a monument honoring the westward expansion of the US.

Producers of the Styx *Arch Allies* disc were James Young and Gary Loizzo. For the REO disc, Cronin and Amato handled production duties with Joe Vannelli, who would also work production on 2002's Christmas song 'I Believe in Santa Claus' for a charity album and continues working with the band today. In 2001, the REO portion of *Arch Allies* was rereleased as

Extended Versions: The Encore Collection and also as *Live Plus*, the latter including three additional tracks. Also in 2001, Cronin appeared on VH1's *Rock 'n' Roll Celebrity Jeopardy*. When he missed a Blue Öyster Cult clue, he responded with, 'Ah, jeez, and I know those guys, too.'

The Songs:
From the second disc featuring REO: 'Don't Let Him Go,' 'Music Man,' 'Take It on the Run,' 'Can't Fight this Feeling,' 'Time for Me to Fly,' 'Back on the Road Again,' 'Keep on Loving You,' 'Roll with the Changes,' 'Ridin' the Storm Out,' '157 Riverside Avenue,' 'Blue Collar Man (Long Nights)' with Styx (Jam Version), 'Roll with the Changes' with Styx (Jam Version)

Related Tracks
'Keep Pushin',' 'Tough Guys,' 'That Ain't Love' (2001)
These three tracks were not on the original *Arch Allies* but did appear with the *Arch Allies* songs on the 2001 release *Live Plus*, a more complete representation of the same 9 June 2000 show.

Find Your Own Way Home (2007)

Kevin Cronin: lead vocals, rhythm guitar
Neal Doughty: keyboards
Bruce Hall: bass guitar, vocals
Dave Amato: lead guitar, vocals
Bryan Hitt: drums, percussion
Bill Hall: clarinet on 'Born to Love You'
Executive Producer: Tom Consolo
Producers: Joe Vannelli, Cronin
Associate Producer: Amato
Engineer: Joe Vannelli
Assistant Engineer: Joe Primeau
Mixing: Joe Vannelli
Mixing Assistant: Scott Cochran
Recorded at Blue Moon Studio
Record Label: Speedwagon Recordings, Mailboat Records
Running Time: 43:59
Released: 3 April 2007
Highest Chart Place: US: –, UK: –

Despite the serious gap between studio records, REO weren't idle or invisible in the late 1990s to mid-2000s. The band continued to tour every year, performing well over 500 shows between *Building the Bridge* and *Find Your Own Way Home*.

Back on 19 January 2001, Governor George Ryan proclaimed REO Speedwagon Day across the state of Illinois. About the same time, the city of Champaign designated a block of Main Street in honor of the band. The honorary REO Speedwagon Way, renewed ten years later but since retired, was in front of the old Vriner's Confectionary (now Memphis on Main), where Marvin Gleicher photographed the band at the counter for the back cover of *R.E.O./T.W.O.*

Later in 2001 REO made their third appearance at Moondance Jam, a weekend festival in Walker, Minnesota, after performing in 1997 and 1999. They would return several more times over the following years. That same year, Amato appeared on Gregg Rolie's (Santana, Journey) *Roots*, contributing backing vocals and guitar.

In the aftermath of the terrorist attacks of 11 September 2001, REO joined Styx to found Rock to the Rescue, a non-profit organization supporting communities across the US. Their first benefit concerts, which included the likes of Foreigner and Bad Company, raised more than $750,000 for families who lost loved ones in the tragedy.

In 2003, Champaign band Ginger reunited and performed at Red Lion, REO's old grounds. Ginger drummer Larry Fredrickson has said that Richrath had served as something of a mentor to Ginger back in the early 1970s. For

117

the 2003 Red Lion show, original REO vocalist Luttrell sat in with Ginger and performed '157 Riverside Avenue.'

REO, along with Styx, Journey, and others, took part in *The Rock n' Roll Holiday Cruise* in December 2004. While some bands showed up at various ports just for their concerts, REO reportedly remained onboard the entire cruise. In addition to the usual touring, 2005 saw Amato contributing guitar work to Ronn Moss' *Uncovered*.

Eventually, it was time for new music. Whatever fans were expecting, it's fair to say they got something better than they'd hoped for. Close to 40 years into the band's history, and more than ten years since their last studio album, it was clear REO hadn't lost it. The record was made at Vannelli's Blue Moon Studio. Vannelli is an extremely talented musician who also happens to be Gino Vannelli's brother. Joe Vannelli produced this album with Cronin, and, for the first time, Amato served as associate producer.

When the band went into the studio, there were no expectations and no pressure, partly because there was no record deal. It was just REO making their own music on their own dime. There's a flow to the album, a theme of working through life's troubles by looking inward, finding strength, and believing in oneself. Perhaps the only let-down was the limited contribution by Doughty. In a 2013 *Classic Rock Revisited* interview with Jeb Wright, Doughty said he was against making a full album at the time because he felt recording just one or two individual songs for digital download made more sense. He also disagreed with some keyboard parts presented to him and 'ended up leaving the project.' Producer Vannelli ably performed in his place, leaving fans to wonder if Doughty was departing the music business. That wasn't the case and Doughty remained with REO until he retired from touring in early 2023.

Find Your Own Way Home was harder rocking than *Building the Bridge*, thanks in part to Amato's growing collection of guitars, and managed to get more airplay. Two of its songs ('I Needed to Fall,' 'Find Your Own Way Home') made it into the Top 25 on *Billboard*'s Adult Contemporary chart for airplay. The CD's front cover featured a slightly battered compass face, its needle pointing about eight degrees west of due north. The back listed the ten tracks next to a great photo of the band, credited to Alex Solca.

As part of the early promotion, the band (minus Doughty) performed on Sirius XM radio's *Artist Confidential* series. In the US, Walmart and Sam's Club had a three-week exclusive on the new CD, packaging it in a limited-edition three-disc set that included their 2006 XM radio 25th anniversary live recording of *Hi Infidelity*, and the aforementioned *Artist Confidential* live DVD with performances of new songs 'Dangerous Combination,' 'I Needed to Fall,' and 'Smilin' in the End.'

The band performed 'The Star Spangled Banner' a cappella at US Cellular Field in Chicago on 2 April 2007 prior to the Cleveland Indians vs Chicago Whitesox baseball game. On 3 April, the same day as *Find Your Own Way Home* was released, St. Louis radio station KSHE inducted REO into its Real

Rock Museum: Hall of Fame. KSHE was one of the earliest supporters of the band, and REO were the first band inducted into KSHE's Hall of Fame. The band was soon touring in Belgium, England, and Scotland, before playing the Sweden Rock Festival in Solvesborg on 9 June 2007. Their hour-long festival set included 'I Needed to Fall' and 'Smilin' in the End.' 14 September 2007 found REO performing at 8:00 am atop a cruise boat traveling on the Chicago River through the city of Chicago, courtesy of radio station WLUP's morning show. The band reworked Van Morrison's classic 'Gloria,' singing 'Johnnnnnny B' (for radio host Jonathon Brandmeier) in place of 'Gloooooooria.'

REO made a television appearance on the CBS Early Show in Greensburg, Kansas, in May 2008, a year after a massive tornado (1.7 miles wide, rated EF-5) struck the area to raise funds for recovery. They performed 'Ridin' the Storm Out' on air, then continued to play for the locals. Anyone in attendance would've heard 'Can't Fight This Feeling,' 'Roll with the Changes,' and 'Find Your Own Way Home.'

In early July 2008, the PBS series *Soundstage* aired *REO Speedwagon: Live in the Heartland*, a 16-song, 90-minute concert recorded in Chicago. New tracks featured were 'Find Your Own Way Home,' 'I Needed to Fall,' 'Dangerous Combination,' and 'Smilin' in the End.' Another benefit performance came on 16 July 2008, when the band headlined the *Ridin' the Storm Out – Floods of 2008 Relief Concert* in Iowa. All proceeds went to Polk County flood victims following several weeks of severe flooding. Also in 2008, Cronin appeared on the American TV show *Don't Forget the Lyrics*, where contestants had to complete popular song lyrics from memory. He made it to the end of the show but was stumped by Donna Summer's 'Last Dance.' Cronin donated his $250,000 winnings to MusiCares. After a short jaunt through Aruba, Trinidad and Tobago, Panama, and Puerto Rico, REO were back touring stateside.

'Smilin' in the End' (Cronin) (3:36)

The CD starts with a true rocker in 'Smilin' in the End,' guitars, bass, and drums grabbing listeners' attention immediately. Cronin's vocals are strong and Amato fires away on guitar on this song about overcoming the odds and proving the naysayers wrong. Cronin sings, 'You can beat me, mistreat me, but guess who'll be smilin' in the end?'

As Cronin mentioned in a May 2016 *Classic Rock* article, when he was starting in the music business and hoping to be a songwriter, he managed to get a meeting with music icon Clive Davis, who'd been president of Columbia Records and was starting up Arista Records. Cronin played Davis some song demos, including very early renditions of 'Can't Fight this Feeling' and 'Time for Me to Fly.' Davis listened, took a pass, and wished Cronin well. Rather than being crushed by the rejection, Cronin dug deep within himself and worked harder. That was part of the inspiration for this song.

REO humor shines through with lyrics like, 'Well, you can leave me cold, I'll recover, say nasty things about my mother.' The song moves loud and fast, the end coming quicker than expected. Doughty plays thunderous organ, his only credit on the album. 'Smilin' in the End' was released to classic rock radio stations in the US the same time 'I Needed to Fall' was released to adult contemporary stations but did not chart.

'Find Your Own Way Home' (Cronin) (4:48)
Cronin composed this following a bleak period while his oldest son was struggling with personal demons. After unsuccessfully trying various ways of helping, Cronin finally adopted the 'tough love' method: 'there is hope for every soul, but I can't wait forever for a miracle.'

The sentiment brings to mind 1978's 'Blazin' Your Own Trail Again.' 'Find Your Own Way Home' grazes ballad territory, but Hitt's drumming adds a punch. There's a certain heartbreak in Cronin's vocals as he forces himself to stand back and watch someone he loves chart his own course, no matter the consequences. But there's a gentle comfort in the 'find your own way home' chorus, rather than a forceful kick out the door. This was the album's third single, making it to number 23 on the US Adult Contemporary chart.

'I Needed to Fall' (Cronin) (4:08)
The track begins with acoustic guitar and Cronin nearly whispering in confidentiality about almost giving up. The lyrics bring to mind 'Headed for a Fall' from 1975's *This Time We Mean It*, about reaching the highs before getting knocked down to new lows. But it also squares nicely with 'Keep on Loving You' and 'Can't Fight this Feeling,' with its theme of finding love, working through overwhelming emotional burdens, growing, and coming back stronger than ever.

The song was somewhat of a struggle to bring to fruition and, at one point, was set aside before the band returned to it (mostly at Amato's suggestion) and finished it. The verses are introspective; the chorus swells and overflows. There's no soloing, but Vannelli adds synth strings and each time the chorus comes around, it's accompanied by big harmonies, loud drums, and heavy guitars. The track was released as a single to US adult contemporary radio stations, reaching 25 on the Adult Contemporary chart.

'Dangerous Combination' (Cronin, Jim Peterik) (4:45)
This is Cronin's second REO song written with Peterik, after 1999's 'Just for You,' but it's not a ballad. Instead, it's a rock tune with modern country influences, about alcohol clouding the lonely narrator's thinking. He's eyeing a certain woman in a bar but knows he should walk away because 'you and me tonight is a dangerous combination.'

Drums and organ push the song and Amato gets to show off lap steel guitar skills. About two-thirds through, he plays a short solo, adding the right twang to the track. The song leaves the listener guessing as to whether the narrator heeds his own warning or leaves with the woman who's 'looking better by the minute.'

'Lost on the Road of Love' (Cronin) (5:16)
Another country-influenced number, 'Lost on the Road to Love' has a light, spunky feel. The song shuffles along loose and easy, making it clear that being lost on the road to love isn't a bad thing. It sounds like something that would've fit with some of Bonnie Raitt's 1980s/early 1990s work. The tune begins on acoustic guitar, Amato's dobro and Hitt's drums soon joining in. Vannelli takes a few turns on the Hammond, trading riffs with the dobro as they weave around the verses. When the instrumental break hits, Vannelli and Amato turn it up and continue trading solos without losing the heart of the song. Gospel-style background vocals add a touch of soul.

'Lost on the Road of Love' winds down with everyone in the band squeezing in a few more licks as the background singers repeat, 'lost, lost on the road of love.' Concert crowd noise is mixed in and Hitt carries the tune home on drums. It's not typical REO but works as part of *Find Your Own Way Home*.

'Another Lifetime' (Amato, Cronin, Hall, Hitt) (4:04)
The only song on the CD with writing credited to most of the band (save Doughty), 'Another Lifetime' starts with loud guitars then drops to a softer mode for the first verse. Here, the song's protagonist is making the difficult decision to walk away from someone he loves because she's decided she can't continue with him. He knows 'in another lifetime, another world,' the two of them could still be together.

Amato churns out gritty riffs and tosses in a brief, snarling solo toward the end of the song, wringing out his last notes at the fade. Vannelli's synth strings provide a nice contrast to the guitar, adding texture to the track.

'Run Away Baby' (Cronin) (3:05)
This one's an amusing, bluesy tune with a bit of wah-wah on top. It's about sneaking off for a little fun, going skinny dipping in a stream, driving 'to a No-Tell motel,' getting a little wild and shaking 'the pictures off the walls.'

But it's more than an amusing, bluesy tune. It's also a lively boogie piece with a touch of rockabilly hiding somewhere within. We get another guitar/keyboard exchange in the midsection, Amato playing clean licks before turning it over to Vannelli on organ, who sends it back to Amato before Cronin returns on vocals. The band is clearly having fun with 'Run Away Baby,' taking the music, but never themselves, seriously.

'Everything You Feel' (Cronin) (5:29)
'Everything You Feel' is a high-octane number that was popping up in the live setlist as far back as 2002. It begins quietly with a moody, atmospheric

introduction, intensifying as guitar, sitar, keyboards, and drums coalesce and crash into 1960s-style pop harmonies telling us, 'You are everything you feel.'

The song continues the theme of finding strength within oneself, acknowledging fears, scars, and excess, and declaring 'you are everything you choose.' Hitt's frantic drumming frames the track. Vannelli lets loose on a brief electric piano solo and Amato presents some toasty extended guitar work, burning the frets, keeping pace with Hitt. When the solo ends, Amato gives us a short acoustic outro to match that moody intro. It's difficult to choose a 'best' song on the CD, but this might be it.

'Born to Love You' (Hall) (4:46)

Hall takes over lead vocals for his 'Born to Love You' blues tune, written for his wife. It's a family affair as Hall's dad Bill helps out on clarinet for the song's introduction. Sadly, Bill passed away not long after recording his part.

Vannelli turns in some deft keyboard work, his piano bringing to mind Ray Charles on a baby grand, and his Hammond providing the wave on which the song rides. Midway, Cronin joins on vocals for the bridge. Background singers provide a soulful edge, especially when they burst out with 'born to love you' and 'heart and soul.' Hall brings the right amount of grit to his singing to give the track a feeling of truth.

'Let My Love Find You' (Cronin) (3:58)

The closing track pulls the listener back into the country-influenced side of *Find Your Own Way Home*. Piano and guitar create a longing feeling and the lyrics read partly like a prayer: 'May your spirit guide you, may it brightly burn.' Cronin's vocals are impassioned and the musical performances are subdued but powerful. It's a perfect end to an album about seeking strength, finding love, and growing each day.

Related release
XM Artist Confidential

The limited-edition release of *Find Your Own Way Home* contained a live 'unplugged' seven-track DVD of REO (minus Doughty) at the XM Performance Theater in Washington, DC. Host George Taylor Morris talked with the band between songs, providing background and stories surrounding the music.

The songs: 'Music Man,' 'Dangerous Combination,' 'Ridin' the Storm Out,' 'I Needed to Fall,' 'Smilin' in the End,' 'Take It on the Run,' and 'Roll with the Changes.' The three songs from the new album would've been new to the audience, since this was recorded before *Find Your Own Way Home* was released. Four songs from the XM show ('Take It on the Run,' 'Smilin' in the End,' 'I Needed to Fall,' 'Ridin' the Storm Out') were included on the European CD as bonus tracks.

Not So Silent Night – Christmas with REO Speedwagon (2009)

Personnel:
Kevin Cronin: lead vocals, rhythm guitar
Bruce Hall: bass guitar, vocals
Neal Doughty: keyboards
Dave Amato: lead guitar, vocals
Bryan Hitt: drums, percussion
Joe Vannelli: orchestration and additional keyboards
Carol Perry, Darlene Perry, Lori Perry, Sharon Perry: backing vocals
Dave Pearlman: pedal steel guitar on 'Blue Christmas'
Mark Goldenberg: acoustic guitar on 'I Believe in Santa Claus' 2010
Holly Cronin: backing vocals on 'I Believe in Santa Claus' 2010
Producer: Joe Vannelli
Associate Producer: Cronin
Engineer: Joe Vannelli
Assistant Engineers: Jeremy Duché, Joe Primeau
Recorded at Blue Moon Studio
Released 4 November 2009; 5 October 2010 with 3 bonus tracks; 3 November 2017 with one additional bonus track previously available only on iTunes plus a rerecorded 'I Believe in Santa Claus' offered for download
Running Time: 45:56 (2009); 56:42 (2010); 60:02 (2017)
Highest Chart Place: US: –, UK: –

A holiday record from REO Speedwagon? The band was almost late to the game with this one, as most rock bands had already released Christmas albums in the 1990s and early 2000s, but it was a welcome addition to the REO canon. It would never be mistaken for an all-out rock fest, as the title implies, but it does bring the classic rock sound to the holidays. REO worked on many of the song demos in 2008, though the definitive recordings came later and the CD wasn't released until late 2009. Most tracks, both secular and traditional/religious, are well-known, but a few obscure gems made the cut, as well as one band original, which had first appeared on a charity compilation in 2002.

Vannelli again produced and engineered after serving the same roles on *Find Your Own Way Home*. This is the last studio album to date from REO, but *Not So Silent Night* has been issued three times. First in 2009, then as an expanded edition in 2010, and again in 2017, expanded further with a song previously available only as a downloadable track in 2010 and a coupon for a downloadable rerecorded version of 'I Believe in Santa Claus.'

Each release had the same sketch of Santa Claus (who perhaps bore a resemblance to Doughty) on the front cover but in different colors. 2009's cover came in blue/grey, while 2010's was red. Those featured a back cover photo of the band along some railroad tracks with bare winter trees in the background. The 2017 front cover had a green tint and, on the back, a photo of the band with their instruments, except Doughty, who's tipping his hat. The 2009 and 2010 versions were on the Sony Music label. Sony, coincidentally, is the home of REO's original record label, Epic. The 2017 rerelease of *Not So Silent Night* was issued on Warner Music Group's Rhino label, which also released the album as a 12-song vinyl LP the same year.

The 2010 edition was available with a companion DVD, one of several holiday records in Sony Legacy's *The Yule Log* series. The DVD did not feature any live performances from the band but consisted of the studio recordings with a choice of three holiday scenes: The Classic Yule Log, The Snowy Cottage, or The Cosy Cottage.

More than anything, *Not So Silent Night* was a gift to the fans and shouldn't be dismissed as a lightweight, clichéd attempt to cash in on the holidays. There's a sense of joy throughout and it sounds and feels like the band had fun putting it together. As part of the tour, in 2010 and early 2011, REO partnered with Abbey Road Live to sell two-CD sets of some of their concerts. Fans could attend the show and then immediately purchase *Live and Limited* – typically limited to 1,000 pressings – from that very show on their way out of the venue.

'The First Noel' (Traditional English Carol) (0:58)
'The First Noel' is a comforting but short take on the traditional tune. Cronin sings it like a lullaby, covering the first two lines ('The first Noel, the angel did say was to certain poor shepherds in fields as they lay') and one refrain of 'Noel, Noel, Noel, Noel, born is the king of Israel.'

The song is believed to have originated in southwest England, its Cornish origins dating back at least to the 1500s. That would make it one of the oldest pieces of music (along with some other tunes on this holiday disc) REO have recorded to date. Cronin's 21st Century vocals are accompanied primarily by piano and sitar, the song rising and swelling for the chorus before gently fading out.

'Winter Wonderland' (Felix Bernard, Dick Smith) (3:03)
After the soft, ballad-like 'The First Noel,' listeners might've been wondering about the 'not so silent' in the album's title. 'Winter Wonderland,' written in 1934, moves closer to classic rock, beginning with a Chuck Berry-type lick and bringing 1950s-style rock and roll to the tune.

REO chose to go with the original lyrics, singing, 'and pretend that he is Reverend Brown' rather than the alternate 1947 lyrics of 'and pretend that he's a circus clown,' which are often combined in 'Winter Wonderland' recordings since the late 1950s. Piano provides a boogie undercurrent, while the chorus backing vocals are made for singing along ('later on,' 'we'll conspire,' 'as we dream,' 'by the fire'). Cronin introduces the guitar break with,

'Alright, Davey,' and Amato's there with a flawless swinging solo that's spot on for the mood of the song.

'Silent Night' (Joseph Mohr, Franz Gruber) (3:43)
Not as old as 'The First Noel,' 'Silent Night' is still a Christmas carol that has stood the test of time, having been composed back in 1818. It was first performed on Christmas Eve in Orberndorf in the Austrian Empire that year.

Here, 'Silent Night' is a power ballad with solid keyboards, punchy drums, and lilting guitar. Backing vocals take the form of a choir, swaying to the music and bringing a majestic feeling to the tune. The track ends with wistful guitar that brings to mind the emotion of 'I Wish You were There' from *Hi Infidelity*. The song reached number 50 on Canada's Adult Contemporary chart in 2010.

'Deck the Halls' (Traditional Welsh Carol) (3:25)
Another holiday tune dating back centuries, the Welsh melody is estimated to be as old as the 1500s, while Thomas Oliphant's English-language lyrics are from 1862. John Jones (Talhaiarn) provided Welsh lyrics around the same time. A slightly revised set of English lyrics appeared in 1877, and it's those lyrics used here. The changes aren't drastic, but, for example, rather than 'Fill the mead cup, drain the barrel,' Cronin sings the more familiar, 'Don we now our gay apparel.'

'Deck the Halls' begins with trumpet notes from the synthesizer and a child saying, 'Wake up, Daddy, I think I heard Santa.' Cronin answers and soon the song shifts into high gear, Trans-Siberian Orchestra style. This is one of the most 'rock' tunes on the CD. It dashes along, capturing the fun and excitement of preparing for the holidays and gathering friends and loved ones together.

'Little Drummer Boy' (Katherine Davis, Henry Onorati, Harry Simeone) (3:49)
'Little Drummer Boy,' sometimes known as 'Carol of the Drum,' was written in 1941. There's no drum solo here (perhaps that would've been too obvious), but Hitt shines, delivering a steady march. Doughty sparkles on piano, keeping pace with Hitt, climbing over and under the drumming. In contrast to the buoyant, exuberant vocals on 'Deck the Halls,' Cronin takes a more solemn tone without ever dragging it down. Bass and guitar support the drumming, and Amato executes some sweet guitar work toward the end of the song.

'The White Snows of Winter' (Bob Shane, Tom Drake, Johannes Brahms) (2:56)
Bob Shane, founding member of the Kingston Trio, co-wrote 'The White Snows of Winter' in 1960. The song first appeared on the Trio's *The Last*

Month of the Year. Songwriting partner Tom Drake was a Canadian child actor, screenwriter, director, and singer/songwriter who wrote lyrics for several Kingston Trio songs in the early 1960s. Shane and Drake based the song around Johannes Brahms' First Symphony.

The singer tells the story of love found but soon left behind as he heads out to sea. When he returns, 'my love cannot be found' though as he sits and asks for another pint, he says, 'my love lies a-sleeping, I know that she is near.' That could be taken two ways. First, he has again found his true love and will be reconciled on Christmas. Or he finds his true love 'a-sleeping,' her gravesite somewhere near, and he will soon be spending eternity with her. In the Christmas spirit, most listeners assume the meaning is the former and the singer and his love will be reunited on Christmas morning. It's a quiet piece, invoking a winter's night as snow falls steadily and blankets everything into silence. Cronin is accompanied by piano and strings, matching the longing of love lost and regained.

'Angels We Have Heard on High (Gloria)' (Traditional French Carol) (4:16)

'Angels We Have Heard on High' was composed in the mid-1800s, the music based on the traditional French carol 'Les Anges dans nos Campagnes' (The Angels in our Countryside). English lyrics were written by Irish-born Roman Catholic priest James Chadwick, based loosely on the French lyrics.

REO's take begins reverentially, with simple but beautiful piano and Cronin singing, 'Angels we have heard on high...' Then the chorus comes in, fostering a bigger sound without losing any sincerity. After that first chorus, Amato shines as he momentarily brings it back down to an uncomplicated carol for a moment before the music swells again. By the midpoint, 'Angels We Have Heard on High' flirts with the power ballad structure and closes out with an unspoken invitation for everyone to join in the chorus.

'Children Go Where I Send Thee' (Traditional African-American Song) (4:04)

Also known as 'Children, Go Where I Send You,' the song has been recorded in nearly every musical genre, including gospel, spiritual, classical, folk, country, and rock, by everyone from Odetta to Johnny Cash. The song is an African-American spiritual with origins to mid-1800s English folk music ('The Twelve Apostles'), and perhaps even further to the 1500s. While some versions of the contemporary song build the verses with a count to twelve, REO stops at ten ('I'm gonna send them ten by ten, ten for Ten Commandments').

The band dives right into this track, a joyous, gospel-tinged boogie complete with sitar. Hitt's drumming drives the song forward at a brisk tempo. The first time the 'five for the gospel' line comes along, the music breaks for a moment as the choir shouts a cappella for one word: 'preachers.' It's a good time with bright background vocals and an exuberant choir.

126

'I'll be Home for Christmas' (Kim Gannon, Walter Kent, Buck Ram) (3:47)

'I'll be Home for Christmas' was composed in 1943 with thoughts in mind of World War II soldiers fighting far away from home. American crooner Bing Crosby was the first to have a hit with it and it's since been recorded by countless others.

REO's version begins on piano. Cronin sings, 'I'll be home, I'll be home for Christmas,' as the background singers echo, 'I'll be home, I'll be home' with a 1950s doo-wop flair. Cronin provides a tongue-in-cheek spoken interlude mid-song: 'Now darlin,' I know I've been on the road...' and mentions walking 'all the way home from Saint Louis' if necessary, to be home for Christmas morning. Guitars twang away as he speaks, adding the right amount of heartbreak.

'God Rest Ye Merry Gentlemen' (Traditional English Carol) (3:51)

Another centuries-old song, 'God Rest Ye (or You) Merry Gentlemen' has been around since the mid-1600s. Like 'Deck the Halls,' this version has a very Trans-Siberian Orchestra vibe. It's unapologetically up-tempo, with lively piano and occasional vocal effects. One surprise is Hall's funky bass interlude, lasting about 35 seconds and sounding like nothing else on the album but fitting in perfectly. Guitar and drums bash away for a bit with unrestrained merriness before Cronin sings about the 'funky gentlemen.' Coincidentally, the male background singers (Amato and Hall) on the album are identified as 'The Funky Gentlemen.'

'Happy Xmas (War is Over)' (John Lennon, Yoko Ono) (4:23)

John Lennon's contemplative Christmas tune was written in 1971 as a protest against the war in Vietnam. There are no surprises or reinterpretations here. REO stay true to the original, well-loved lament from Lennon and Yoko Ono. 'So this is Christmas,' say the lyrics, asking in the season of peace and love, 'and what have you done?'

It opens with melancholy piano, providing a sharp contrast with the raucousness of 'God Rest Ye Merry Gentlemen.' Cronin enters on vocals and the song slowly escalates, with the rest of the band and background singers coming in. A mandolin enhances the later verses. As the song fades out, Cronin adds, 'We love you, John. Rest in peace.'

'Blue Christmas' (Billy Hayes, Jay W. Johnson) (3:57)

'Blue Christmas' was written in 1948 and is most often associated with Elvis Presley, though Ernest Tubb and other musicians had success with it before Presley. On this track, the band bring in Dave Pearlman on pedal steel guitar. Pearlman founded and ran a recording studio in California for more than 25 years and currently builds high-end custom microphones. As a studio musician, he's worked with Chuck Berry, Dan Fogelberg, Terry Reid, and others.

Hall takes lead vocals, with Pearlman providing a country lilt. When Hall sings, 'I'll have a blue Christmas without you,' he gives it the full crying-in-your-beer, all-alone-for-the-holidays treatment. There's a gentle sadness carried throughout the song that somehow still leaves the listener smiling.

'Joy to the World' (Isaac Watts, George Frideric Handel) (3:43)
Isaac Watts, an English minister, wrote the words to 'Joy to the World' in 1719. It was American Lowell Mason who later coupled the words with Handel's 'Antioch' to give us the carol we recognize today. Watts' lyrics were based on Psalm 98 ('make a joyful noise unto the Lord').

After the lonesomeness of 'Blue Christmas,' REO veer back into rock territory with this mid-tempo number. It fades in on Amato's sustained guitar note, drums, bass, piano, and sitar elevating it before Cronin sings the first line. Background singers provide a nod to Handel with their choir support. The instrumental break toward the latter part of the song provides a chance to stretch out. Piano notes cascade down the keyboard, sitar and organ take the spotlight for a bit, electric guitar wails, while the background singers 'feel the joy.'

'Sleigh Ride' (Mitchell Parish, Leroy Anderson) (3:47)
Leroy Anderson wrote the music for 'Sleight Ride' in 1948, when it was performed as an instrumental, notably by the Boston Pops Orchestra. Mitchell Parish added lyrics two years later. The song begins with inviting bass and drums, organ swirling in before the first verse begins: 'Just hear those sleigh bells jingling.' The band sticks with the original lyric of 'there's a birthday party at the home of Farmer Gray,' rather than the sometimes substituted 'there's a Christmas party at the home of Farmer Gray.' All the while, Hitt's drums mimic the gait of horses drawing a sleigh through the snow. It's a lively take on an energetic song.

'Hark! The Herald Angels Sing' (Charles Wesley, Felix Mendelssohn) (4:12)
English Methodist cleric Charles Wesley drafted the words for 'Hark! The Herald Angels Sing' in 1739, based on the Bible's Luke 2:14 ('Glory to God in the highest heaven and on earth peace among those he favors'). A century later, it was paired with the music of 'Vaterland, in deinen Gauen,' an excerpt of Felix Mendelssohn's 'Gutenberg Cantata.' The band take their time playing on this one. It's a sincere ballad, with a small choir of background vocalists adding a majestic touch.

'I Believe in Santa Claus' (Cronin, Hall) (2:45)
The sole original composition on the CD, 'I Believe in Santa Claus' has surfaced in several iterations. It was first on a charity compilation disc in 2002. A rerecorded version was released as a single in 2009, then that

recording was included on the 2010 and 2017 rereleases of *Not So Silent Night*. Finally, a new version of the track was downloadable with the 2017 rerelease.

The song's genesis is an incident from Cronin's childhood. As he writes in the album notes, at age six, a friend said he didn't believe in Santa. This version of the song begins with acoustic guitar and 'ooh, ooh, I believe' background vocals, creating a sense of innocence before starting the first verse: 'Me and a friend in the neighborhood, playing in the snow.' The 'me and a friend' grammar immediately creates a childhood setting. It tells of counting down days to Christmas and flying reindeer. There's a gentle sway to the music that evokes holiday comfort. And, of course, Santa is real. 'I believe anything is possible, I believe in miracles,' sings Cronin.

The 2017 rerelease contains the same recording of 'I Believe in Santa Claus,' but a coupon allows for a download of a reworked version of the track. The downloadable track (clocking in at 3:38) begins with a few shakes of sleigh bells and electric guitar. The words and melody are consistent, though this version has more guitar and begins with the full chorus of 'I believe' before the first verse of 'me and a friend.'

'We Three Kings' (John Henry Hopkins, Jr) (3:21)
John Henry Hopkins, Jr, rector of a church in Pennsylvania, composed 'We Three Kings' (also known as 'Three Kings of Orient') in 1857. Hopkins wrote it for a Christmas pageant while attending seminary in New York City. REO originally made this available only as a downloadable track but later added it to the 2017 rerelease. The song begins quietly on piano and guitar, a plaintiveness underscoring the beauty of the composition. Midway through, the chorus is presented canon-style, with Cronin providing accompaniment to his own vocals. There's an earnest, weary feeling to 'We Three Kings,' with Cronin's heartrending vocals and Amato's guitar crying into the night, reflecting a long, exhausting sojourn with a sublime ending.

Related Tracks
'I Believe in Santa Claus' from *A Classic Rock Christmas* (Cronin, Hall) (2002) (3:38)
The band first recorded 'I Believe in Christmas' for a charity holiday compilation in 2002. The song is essentially the same as what later appeared on *Not So Silent Night,* but with a few differences, notably a slightly longer intro and a few measures of 'Santa Claus is Coming to Town' nestled in about two-thirds of the way through. Like the other versions, a sense of innocence and optimism permeate. It's easy to picture a cozy gathering around a fireplace, warm memories and recollections flowing as snow falls outside in the quiet night.

Cronin and Hall wrote it, with Cronin and Vannelli producing. It was recorded at Blue Moon Studio, where *Find Your Way Own Home, Not So*

Silent Night and 'Can't Stop Rockin'' with Styx would later be recorded. After being difficult to find for some time, the band posted the track on its website, with a spoken introduction added over the first instrumental measures of music. Cronin says, 'Hi everybody, this is Kevin Cronin from REO Speedwagon wishing you a happy holiday season and a rockin' new year from all your friends right here at speedwagon-dot-com.'

Live at Moondance Jam (2013)

Personnel:
Kevin Cronin: lead vocals, rhythm guitar
Neal Doughty: keyboards
Bruce Hall: bass guitar, lead vocals on 'Back on the Road Again'
Dave Amato: lead guitar
Bryan Hitt: drums
Executive Producer: Tom Consolo
Producer: Joe Vannelli
Record Label: Frontiers Records
Running Time: 75:31
Highest Chart Place: US: –, UK: –

REO wrapped up their 'Can't Stop Rockin'' tour with Styx in 2010, and that June hit the road with Pat Benatar for the 'Love on the Run' tour. In July, they appeared for the sixth time at Moondance Jam in Walker, Minnesota. By the end of the year, REO were firmly into their 'Hi Infidelity 30th Anniversary' tour. Throughout 2011, the band kept busy. Hitt performed on Stan Bush's *Stan Bush & Barrage*. Cronin took part in the Country Music Hall of Fame and Museum's All for the Hall Los Angeles benefit to raise funds to expand the museum. He played 'Music Man,' 'Keep on Loving You,' and 'In My Dreams.' In 2012 REO toured with Styx and Ted Nugent (Amato's former bandmate) on the 'Midwest Rock n' Roll Express' tour. In March, Cronin appeared on the Canadian show *Star Academie*. Doughty performed on Concentual's EP *File Under: Rock 'n Roll, Vol 1*. Sometime in 2012, the house immortalized in '157 Riverside Avenue' was torn down; another house was built on the same site.

Long-time REO guitar tech and road crew manager Brad 'Porque' Baker passed away in August 2012. In addition to forming and performing in Hotel Bill and the Incidentals, Porque developed and guided the Itchycoo Park Music Festival in Tennessee, and later the Bonaroo Festival.

That November, gibson.com reported REO had recently been in Nashville to start work on a new album, recording the track 'Nothing We Can't Rise Above.' Nothing further was mentioned about a new studio album.

REO's July 2010 appearance at Moondance in front of 30,000 fans was captured for this 2013 release. Accompanying the CD was a DVD of the same show. By the time of the recording, this line-up had been together for more than 20 years and it shows in the tightness and confidence in the performances. A venue like this requires a 'best of' setlist, and REO delivered. The only let-down is that there is nothing from the Amato/Hitt albums. For that matter, *Life as We Know It* isn't represented, nor is *Good Trouble* (which is standard), but it's difficult to whittle more than a dozen studio albums down to a 90-minute show.

The DVD begins with a view of the stage setup. A video screen in the background shows an old hi-fi system with *Hi Infidelity* spinning on a turntable before the band tears into 'Don't Let Him Go.' Hitt easily nails the drum sound and feel of the original. From there, the concert builds and leads into a few more tracks from side one of *Hi Infidelity*, for which the band was celebrating the album's 30th anniversary. Cronin gives a few of his patented talks and introductions to the classic tracks, while all band members seem primed for the show, turning in energetic and joyful performances. As the DVD fades out, a snippet of 'Smilin' in the End' from *Find Your Own Way Home* plays over the credits.

The Songs:
'Don't Let Him Go,' 'Keep on Loving You,' 'In Your Letter,' 'Take It on the Run,' 'Keep Pushin',' 'Golden Country,' 'Can't Fight this Feeling,' 'Like You Do,' 'Time for Me to Fly,' 'Back on the Road Again,' 'Roll with the Changes,' 'Ridin' the Storm Out,' '157 Riverside Avenue.'

Related Tracks
'Can't Stop Loving You (Unfinished Poem)' (Cronin) (2009) [Unreleased]
Performed as early as 2009 in concert, the acoustic ballad tells of a lonely man falling in love with a woman he can't have: 'I was nobody's lover and you were somebody's girl.' The two soon say their last goodbyes. Through his tears, he accepts his fate but admits, 'there can be no fairy tale ending, just an unfinished poem.'

'Nothing We Can't Rise Above' (Cronin, Jonathan Cain, Chris Lindsey) (2012) [Unreleased]
This is the track REO reportedly recorded during a trip to Nashville in late 2012, the first to be worked on for a new studio album. A co-write by Cronin, Journey's Jonathan Cain, and country music writer and producer Chris Lindsey, the song about relationships has never been released, nor has there been any further news of the proposed studio album.

Can't Stop Rockin' – REO On the Road from 2013

REO Speedwagon's last full set of studio material hit the market in 2009 and the Moondance CD was released in 2013, but REO haven't slowed down. They also reportedly visit Blue Moon Studio now and then to record new music, but nothing's been released. The timeline below is nowhere near all-inclusive but provides a glimpse of the past ten or so years.

2013

On 20 January, at Nashville, Tennessee's EXIT/IN, the Tons o' Fun band, with original REO singer Terry Luttrell, performed a memorial show celebrating Brad 'Porque' Baker's life. Joining Tons o' Fun on stage for a rousing, horn-saturated, eight-minute version of '157 Riverside Avenue' were Doughty, Gratzer, Cronin, and Hall, along with former REO roadies and Incidentals James 'Motor' Merritt and Bub Phillippe. Luttrell and Cronin traded vocals on '157 Riverside Avenue.'

Doughty performed on two more EPs by the band Concentual: *Music is the Weapon of the Future* and *Listen Out Loud*. Hitt played on Jef Scott's *Ten Stories*. The 'Midwest Rock n' Roll Express' returned with REO, Styx, and Nugent. Rock to the Rescue collected thousands for charities along the tour and raised over $100,000 for the Boston One Fund to help victims of the 2013 Boston Marathon bombings.

On 9 September, Cronin performed at House of Blues in Chicago at the unveiling of Marco Nunes' Great Chicago Fire Hydrant public art project. The project generated 101 five-foot-tall hydrants, one for each fire station in the city, with Cronin sponsoring an artist. After public display around the city, fire hydrants were then to be auctioned to support fallen firefighter and police families. Cronin's intimate performance included 'Take it on the Run,' 'Time for Me to Fly,' 'Keep on Loving You,' and 'Roll with the Changes.'

On 4 December, REO played another Rock to the Rescue benefit, this time for victims of tornados and storms in central Illinois earlier in the year. The line-up included Head East, Styx, Survivor, Richard Marx, and Ted Nugent, and Hall's friend, comedian Larry the Cable Guy. The evening's biggest surprise occurred when guitarist Richrath joined the band for 'Ridin' the Storm Out.' Richrath remained on stage for the encore 'With a Little Help from My Friends.' It would be his last performance with REO.

2014

REO returned to Moondance Jam in Minnesota in July. That summer also saw REO tour with Chicago. Each did a shorter set, then returned to the stage together. Fans were treated to 'Keep on Loving You,' 'Roll with the Changes,' 'Ridin' the Storm Out,' and more with horns. REO performed on Chicago songs like 'Does Anybody Really Know What Time It Is?' and '25 or 6 to 4.' Over the year, REO debuted a new Cronin song, 'Whipping Boy,' in the live setlist. In December, Amato was part of *Raiding the Rock Vault* in Las Vegas, Nevada, performing tunes like 'Jukebox Hero' and 'Highway to Hell.' The show is an ongoing full concert tribute to the history of rock and roll performed in a club setting.

2015

Early in 2015, Amato returned to *Raiding the Rock Vault*. In May, REO appeared with Imagine Dragons on American TV show *Jimmy Kimmel Live!*, performing 'Roll with the Changes' under the moniker Imagine REO SpeeDragons. The 'Family First' tour saw REO scheduling shows in a way that allowed them to spend more time with their families. On stage, Amato often took lead vocal duties on Nugent's 'Stranglehold.'

On 13 September, Gary Richrath passed away at age 65 following medical complications. Two nights later, in Augusta, Georgia, at REO's next scheduled show, Cronin walked out on stage alone to announce Richrath's passing. It was Richrath who brought Cronin into REO. Cronin said, 'I learned everything I know about being in a rock band from Gary Richrath' and added, 'I love the man. We had our ups and down through the years, but he holds a place in my heart that is so special.' Cronin dedicated 'this show and probably every show we ever play in the future' to Richrath.

Less than a week later, *CMT Crossroads* featured REO and country singer/songwriter Sara Evans. Together they played 'Roll with the Changes,' 'Keep on Loving You,' and 'Take it On the Run.' Cronin and Evans performed Evans' 'A Real Fine Place to Start.'

On 9 November, Richrath's son Eric joined REO in Champaign to perform 'Ridin' the Storm Out.' Original singer Luttrell then joined the band for '157 Riverside Avenue.' On 13 November, KSHE hosted its 48th Birthday Party at the Peabody Opera House in St. Louis, Missouri. Early REO guitarist Scorfina performed slide guitar with Danny Liston (Mama's Pride) & Friends to open the show. Scorfina said he was treated very well by REO, who were 'absolutely fantastic' toward him. When he stepped on stage with Liston, Scorfina started by playing 'a few licks for my friend, Gary Richrath' before diving into Muddy Waters' 'Trouble No More.'

2016

On 15 February, the 58th Annual Grammy Awards included Richrath in their 'In Memoriam' segment.

Later in 2016, Doughty contributed honky-tonk piano on The Easthills' 'Holiday Women' from their *Fear and Temptation* CD. REO sang the national anthem a cappella on 4 July prior to the New York Yankees vs Chicago White Sox game at US Cellular Field (formerly Comiskey Park) in Chicago. Around the same time, REO performed 'Messin' Around' with Pitbull on American TV show *Greatest Hits*.

On 7-8 October, Red Lion in Champaign celebrated its 50th anniversary with a music bash. REO used Red Lion as a rehearsal space in the early years, wrote much of the first album there, and played hundreds of shows at the venue. Guitarist Scorfina's band Soul Steel performed, as did singer Luttrell with Tons o' Fun. When Tons o' Fun performed '157 Riverside Avenue,' Scorfina joined on slide guitar.

    REO couldn't make the Red Lion party due to their tour with Def Leppard and Tesla but sent an 11-minute concert clip from Eugene, Oregon. During the extended intro to 'Back on the Road,' Cronin told the crowd, 'There's a little bar down in Champaign, Illinois, called the Red Lion. The Red Lion was the place where everybody used to play back in the day. And the first time that I ever heard Bruce (Hall) sing this next song, he was jammin' on stage with his own band, The One-Eyed Jacks. And he was singing the song he's gonna sing for you right now. That was 1972.' Cronin added, 'If it wasn't for the Red Lion, I'm not sure where we would be today because they gave us our start... Put your hands together for the Red Lion in Champaign!'

    Later in October, Amato appeared at the Gibson Showroom studio in Las Vegas, Nevada, performing 'Roll with the Changes' for KVVU Fox5. Toward the end of the year, REO toured the UK, opening for Status Quo. The final show, on 23 December, was in Liverpool, where REO performed The Beatles' 'I Saw Her Standing There.'

2017

January found REO on the Rock Legends Cruise. Also on the cruise were Derek St. Holmes (Ted Nugent) and Don Felder (The Eagles). Amato sat in with Felder on 'Hotel California.' St. Holmes joined REO for 'Stranglehold.' Also in January, Amato and Hitt joined St. Holmes at the Midnight Mission Benefit Show in Camarillo, California, raising funds to help the homeless. Included in their performance were Nugent's 'Cat Scratch Fever' and 'Stranglehold,' and The Doors' 'Roadhouse Blues.'

    On 4 April, Amato and Cronin, with Cronin on acoustic guitar, sang the national anthem at Guaranteed Rate Field (formerly US Cellular Field) for the Detroit Tigers vs Chicago White Sox baseball game. This was at least the third time band members performed the anthem at a White Sox game. In June, REO hit the road with Styx and Don Felder for the *United We Rock* tour. Amato played 'Hotel California' with Felder every night.

    After being 'stuck' at sales of 9,000,000 since 1995, *Hi Infidelity* hit diamond status in the US, reaching the 10,000,000 sales milestone in August. One of the band's diamond award plaques is currently housed at the Illinois Rock and Roll Museum in Joliet, Illinois.

2018

In February, Cronin and Amato took part in Rock and Roll Fantasy Camp in Los Angeles, teaching and jamming with dedicated fans. Later in the year, REO toured again with Styx and Don Felder.

    Carolyn Conroy, who'd been friends with REO from their early days and remained a friend of Richrath through the years, started working on a memorial to the guitarist. She and others from the Remembering Gary Richrath Facebook group sold t-shirts with Richrath's image and the line 'There'll never be another' to raise funds.

2019
REO donated proceeds from two shows at Fred Kavli Theater in California to benefit those affected by the 7 November 2018 shootings at the Borderline Bar and Grill and by the recent Woolsey and Hill wildfires. Originally scheduled for one show on 12 January as part of their regular tour, the band turned it into a benefit and added a second show on the 13th, with Eddie Money and Richard Marx joining the cause. Cronin's daughter Holly performed at the concerts, as did Cronin's sons' band Sir, Please.

In early 2019, Cronin toured with *Rock Meets Classic* in Europe, where classic rock hits are performed with the Mat Sinner band and the Bohemian Symphony Orchestra Prague. Cronin's time on stage included 'Take It on the Run,' 'Can't Fight this Feeling,' 'Roll with the Changes,' and 'Keep on Loving You.' Also on the bill were Ian Gillan (Deep Purple) and Mike Reno (Loverboy). Cronin and Reno joined Gillan for the encore of 'Smoke on the Water.' Reno and Cronin would appear together again on tour in 2022.

Guitarist Scorfina joined singer Luttrell on stage 8 March at The Wildey Theater in Edwardsville, Illinois, near St. Louis, to perform '157 Riverside Avenue,' with Scorfina on slide guitar. The two would've also done 'Gypsy Woman's Passion' from the first REO album if they'd had more time to rehearse.

In early June, the Gary Richrath memorial bench was unveiled in River Front Park on Riverside Drive in East Peoria, Illinois. The golden-colored bench proved a fitting tribute. For a time, Richrath had a ranch in Malibu, California. There was a bench there and friend Carolyn Conroy said, 'When he wanted to think and be alone, that's where he would go.'

Later in June, Hall's daughter Sara's band Upshot opened the show for REO at the Virginia Theater in Champaign. Original drummer Gratzer attended REO's 20 August show in Livermore, California, near Sacramento. Gibson released the Dave Amato Les Paul Axcess Standard guitar. On 13 September, REO performed at Kaaboo festival in San Diego, California. At the suggestion of Hitt, they played 'Two Tickets to Paradise' in honor of friend Eddie Money who'd passed away earlier that day. 'Two Tickets to Paradise' made the live setlist regularly for a time afterward.

The Bob Nutt/Blytham Ltd. Tribute Concert was held on 28 September at Champaign's Virginia Theater, following Nutt's passing on 3 September. Nutt, with Irving Azoff, booked all of REO's shows in the late 1960s and early 1970s through Blytham Ltd. Among the many performers at the concert were early REO members Scorfina and Luttrell.

In October, Amato performed on Greg Rolie's *Sonic Ranch*. Cronin appeared on *Songwriters Under the Covers with Victoria Shaw*, filmed at

New York's Birdland Theater. The episode aired on 20 November and featured Sara Evans, who'd performed with REO on CMT *Crossroads* in 2015. Cronin sang 'Keep on Loving You,' 'Take It on the Run,' and 'Roll with the Changes.' He sat in on Shaw's 'Ten Mistakes' and Evans' 'Born to Fly' and 'Marquee Sign.'

2020

Amato performed at the Ronnie Montrose tribute concert on 17 January. Later that month, Amato and Cronin returned to Rock and Roll Fantasy Camp. On 20 February, Amato and Cronin appeared at the Eddie Money Tribute concert in Beverly Hills, performing 'I Think I'm in Love.'

Early in the year, singer Michael Murphy from the mid-1970s REO line-up was the victim of a hit and run accident in Sherman Oaks, California, and was placed in a medically induced coma for more than a month to aid his recovery. Fortunately, Murphy was back performing by 2022.

By mid-March, REO, like all touring acts, canceled all concerts indefinitely due to the spread of the Covid-19 virus. At the end of March, REO appeared on the Netflix show *Ozark*, performing 'Time for Me to Fly.' After the episode, titled 'Kevin Cronin was Here,' aired, 'Time for Me to Fly,' 'Keep on Loving You,' 'Can't Fight this Feeling,' and 'Take It on the Run' reentered various *Billboard* charts. At the end of the year, Cronin performed, via video, 'Keep Pushin'' for Love You Madly Santa Cruz Fire Relief on 23 December.

2021

Cronin and Amato performed at Sammy Hagar's Acoustic-4-A-Cure show on 15 May. Cronin and Amato played 'Take It on the Run' and 'Roll with the Changes,' later joining Hagar's Wabos for 'Mas Tequila.' The Illinois Rock and Roll Museum inducted its first class on 30 August. Artists included Chicago, Cheap Trick, Ides of March, and REO Speedwagon. From REO, only Cronin made the ceremony, where he performed a solo acoustic 'Keep on Loving You,' before being joined by the six-piece The Millennials on 'Roll with the Changes' and 'Ridin' the Storm Out.'

In June, Amato started his 'Gear Candy' video series, talking about his guitar collection, which numbers well over 150. Around that same time, the band booked the Thousand Oaks Civic Plaza for two weeks to rehearse for their upcoming tour. On 1 July, Richard Irvin, Mayor of Aurora, Illinois, presented the Key to the City to REO 'for unlocking live music.' REO's sold-out show at RiverEdge Park was the first at the venue following its closure of more than a year due to the Covid pandemic. Support act was Head East.

On 28 July, REO and Styx were the inaugural show at the new Hartford Health Care Amphitheater in Bridgeport, Connecticut. REO also received the Key to the City of Bridgeport, where they recorded their first album. At their 25 August New York State Fair appearance, REO pulled in the tenth largest crowd ever for the fair, one of only 12 concerts to surpass 30,000 attendees there. In September, opening act on several shows was Sir, Please (featuring Cronin's sons).

2022

In January, Amato sat out shows until the 16 February gig in Salina, Kansas, due to a positive Covid test. Producer Vannelli filled in on keyboards. The concerts were more 'unplugged' than the usual shows. In late May, REO joined Styx and Loverboy for the 'Live and UnZoomed' tour. In August when Loverboy sat out several shows due to Covid, REO performed 'Working for the Weekend.'

Early June found Amato, Doughty, and Cronin attending the second Illinois Rock and Roll Museum induction ceremony. Cronin inducted the late Gary Loizzo (American Breed). Loizzo had worked with Styx for several decades, as well as with Cronin, and with Survivor. In tribute, Cronin, Amato, Doughty, and Jim Peterik joined others to perform Loizzo's 'Bend Me, Shape Me.' Also being inducted into the Museum that night for songwriting was the late Chuck Berry. For the evening's finale, Cronin and Amato performed 'Johnny B. Goode' with Charles Berry, Jr. With them onstage were Peterik on guitar and Illinois Rock and Roll Museum founder and executive director Ron Romero on bass.

In July, REO were presented the Key to City of Enumclaw, Washington. As it turns out, Mayor Jan Molinaro's grandmother and Cronin's wife's grandmother were sisters. That evening, REO performed at White River Amphitheater in nearby Auburn, Washington.

Following a lengthy illness, original bassist Gregg Philbin passed away on 24 October, with wife Lida at his side. Philbin was included in November's Rock and Roll Hall of Fame 'In Memoriam' tribute, which featured a photo from the early days provided by Arnie White.

2023

On 4 January, fans got a shock when founding member/keyboardist Doughty announced his retirement from touring, albeit with a promise to join the band on select shows. Doughty's replacement was Derek Hilland (Whitesnake, Foreigner, Iron Butterfly, Rick Springfield). REO appeared (with Doughty) on the American storyteller show *The Song* on 7 January performing 'Roll with the Changes,' 'Building the Bridge,' and 'Keep on Loving You.' Hall's son's band Levon provided backing vocals and mandolin.

Despite Doughty's retirement, REO showed no signs of slowing down, hitting the road on 11 January with scores of shows scheduled for the year. 'Building the Bridge' was back in the setlist.

Related Tracks

'Whipping Boy' (Cronin) (2014) [Unreleased]

REO started adding this rock tune to the setlist in 2014. The first time it was performed in public, it was so new that Cronin had a teleprompter on standby to help with the lyrics. The song features stellar work from Hall and Amato. Despite being new, its 'whoa, whoa' refrain is inviting enough for crowds to sing along with. The song conveys the belief that whether it's in a personal relationship or in society in general, people want – and deserve – to be treated with respect and dealt with as equals.

'Messin' Around' by Pitbull and REO (Richrath, Armando Pérez, Enrique Iglesias, Jose Garcia, Jorge Gomez, AJ Junior, Jimmy Thornfeldt, Michael Calderon) (2016) (3:46)
Pitbull's 'Messin' Around,' originally recorded with Enrique Iglesias, features the lyric and melody of 'heard it from a friend, who heard it from a friend, who heard it from another you been messin' around' from 'Take It on the Run.' REO joined Pitbull to perform it on the TV program *Greatest Hits*. It's a twist on the original track, with the protagonist proudly proclaiming, 'I been messin' around.' The performance was later released as a downloadable track.

L.A. is Mine by Richrath Project 3:13 (2021)
Longtime bandmate and collaborator Michael Jahnz worked with Richrath through the 1990s and into the 2000s, releasing *Only the Strong Survive* in 1992 and performing more than a thousand shows with him. Toward the end of the 2010s, Jahnz started sifting through old recordings and working on songs that became *L.A. is Mine*. The band name '3:13' came about as Jahnz and Richrath often worked late into the night, losing track of time and looking up to find it was already 3:13 am. *L.A. is Mine* contains three tracks featuring the late Richrath's guitar work. Project 3:13 (Dennis Pockets on guitar, Scott Weber on Keyboards, Doug Janssen on bass, Andy Crownover on drums alongside Jahnz) also recorded two songs in tribute to Richrath: 'Son of a Poor Man' and 'Ridin' the Storm Out.' The Richrath tracks:

'Help Me Save Me from Myself' (Richrath, Jahnz) (4:02)
The track 'pretty much in a nutshell is Gary's life,' said Jahnz. It's about reaching out to make it through the tough times and struggles in life. It's not a cry for pity, merely a call for help and understanding. Richrath lays down a piercing guitar solo, playing with heart and soul.

'L.A. is Mine' (Richrath, Jahnz) (4:19)
'L.A. is Mine' was started in the early 1970s as Richrath was flying into Los Angeles for the first time, seeing the city below him and dreaming of what might await. The song begins acoustically with Richrath on 12-string. Halfway through, it shifts into an electric rocker, with Crownover pounding away on the drumkit as the entire band kicks into high gear. 'It's an anthem to (Richrath) and his guitar playing,' said Jahnz. 'On the demos he plays forever and ever,' but Jahnz worked hard to edit it down while capturing the essence

of it all. Indeed, there is some truly phenomenal soloing for the last minute or so of the song.

'These Nights' (Richrath Jahnz) (3:35)
The third song featuring Richrath's playing on the CD is a catchy, upbeat rock tune. It's about being on the road with the band, 'guitar in hand' and all that time away from home 'will only make me love you more.' The guitar solo is on the aggressive side, putting a bite into the music but never distracting from the loose, fun vibe. It's a pleasure to hear these tracks with Richrath's touch and fans will be grateful to Jahnz and the band for taking the time to work on them.

'Building the Bridge' (Live) (Cronin) (2023) (4:32)
Taken from the band's January appearance on *The Song* in Nashville, 'Building the Bridge' was made available for download and streaming in early 2023. It's performed with a slightly different arrangement from the original studio version, giving it a fuller feeling. In addition to Doughty on organ, Joe Vannelli assists on piano and Hall's son's band Levon handle backing vocals. Amato's solo is short but powerful and the entire band plays with conviction. It makes for a rich recording and may be enough to entice listeners hearing the song for the first time to seek out the original 1996 *Building the Bridge* studio album.

Additional Compilations and Live Releases

REO's catalog includes innumerable retrospectives. The list below is in addition to *The Hits*, *The Ballads*, and the *Decade* releases, but is not all-encompassing.

Best Foot Forward: The Best of REO Speedwagon (Epic) (1985)
Released outside the US, it was the first REO record with 'Wherever You're Goin' (It's Alright),' from *The Goonies* soundtrack. The album contains twelve tracks total from 1976 to 1985, with five from *Hi Infidelity* but nothing from *Good Trouble*.

Take It on the Run (Columbia) (2000)
A more comprehensive collection than *Best Foot Forward*, this one stretches from 1972 ('Golden Country') through 1984 ('One Lonely Night'). It contains 15 songs, including some that are well-known but not outright hits. The big ones are here ('Keep on Loving You,' 'Can't Fight this Feeling'), but so are numbers like '157 Riverside Avenue (live),' and 'Lightning.' It's one of the first retrospectives to include a tune from *Good Trouble* ('Keep the Fire Burnin''). *Take It on the Run* didn't chart, but it did earn a silver certification in the UK.

Extended Versions: The Encore Collection (BMG Special Products) (2001)
Extended Versions is a successful budget series from BMG that repackages live tracks from earlier releases. This is taken from *Arch Allies*, with the songs in a slightly different running order. It never charted but was certified gold in the US in April 2006.

Live Plus (CMC International, Sanctuary Records) (2001)
Consisting of the REO half of *Arch Allies*, it includes three additional tracks from the same show ('Keep Pushin'',' 'Tough Guys,' 'That ain't Love').

The Essential REO Speedwagon (Epic Legacy) (2004)
A highly recommended two-disc set that covers the Epic years, plus one track from *Building the Bridge*. It's an excellent introduction of the band through the years, even if a few of the songs have already appeared on multiple compilations. It includes tracks from the Luttrell and Murphy years, though not represented is *This Time We Mean It*. This was rereleased in 2009 as a limited edition with a third disc of eight additional tracks from the Cronin years.

Playlist: The Very Best of REO Speedwagon (Epic Legacy) (2008)
A decent 14-track collection culled from 10 albums, with songs up to and including 'Here with Me' from *The Hits*. All tracks are from the Cronin years.

141

Setlist: The Very Best of REO Speedwagon LIVE (2010)

Setlist consists of live tracks, half of which are from *You Get What You Play For* and *Second Decade*, with additional previously unreleased live recordings. A highlight is the first official appearance of the band performing Chuck Berry's 'Johnny B. Goode' from January 1985 in Indianapolis. Several line-ups are represented, with Philbin on bass on three songs, the Amato/Hitt line-up on two others, and the rest with Gratzer, Richrath, Cronin, Doughty, and Hall.

The Box Set Series (Epic Legacy) (2014) (US and Canada release)

A value-priced 4-disc compilation of 42 songs from their Epic years. This was the first release to include the version of 'Ridin' the Storm Out' with Cronin's original vocals (replaced by Murphy's when the *Ridin' the Storm Out* album was released in 1973). That particular Cronin recording also surfaced later on *The Early Years 1971-1977*.

This is a comprehensive overview of the band's first 25 years, from *R.E.O. Speedwagon* through *The Ballads*, with a few oversights. There's just one Murphy vocal, and *This Time We Mean It* isn't represented. On the plus side, it doesn't ignore *Good Trouble*; four cuts from that album appear. It also includes 'Here with Me' from *The Hits* and 'Just for You' from *The Ballads*.

The Early Years 1971-1977 (Sony Music, HNE Recordings, Cherry Red) (2018)

This set contains eight CDs of the first seven albums: *R.E.O. Speedwagon*, *R.E.O./T.W.O.*, *Ridin' the Storm Out*, *Lost in a Dream*, *This Time We Mean It*, *R·E·O*, and the full *Live – You Get What You Play For* spread across two discs. Bonus tracks include edits of single releases, the original Cronin vocal studio versions of 'Ridin' the Storm Out' and 'Son of a Poor Man,' and a previously unreleased live 'Keep Pushin'' from the 1976 tour.

The Classic Years 1978-1990 (Sony Music, HNE Recordings, Cherry Red) (2018)

A companion to *The Early Years*, this nine-CD set continues chronicling REO's output on Epic (now part of Sony Music). It contains *You Can Tune a Piano, but You Can't Tuna Fish, Nine Lives, Hi Infidelity, Hi Infidelity Bonus Tracks, Good Trouble, Wheels are Turnin,' Life as We Know It, The Earth, a Small Man, His Dog and a Chicken*, and *Live 1980-1990*.

Bonus tracks across the CDs include radio/single edits, two live tracks from *Decade*, the *Live Again* radio show previously available only as a promotional vinyl release, *The Goonies* 'Wherever You're Goin' (It's Alright),' and the 'new' songs from *The Hits* and *The Ballads*. The *Hi Infidelity Bonus Tracks* consist of the Crystal Demos, radio edits of singles, live tracks, and the reggae 'Keep on Loving You' from *Second Decade*. The *Live 1980-1990* disc contains ten live recordings from *Second Decade* and seven tracks that appeared on *Setlist LIVE*.

Above: Honorary REO Speedwagon Way. The City of Champaign, Illinois, pays tribute to their local heroes. (*Author*)

Below: The Gary Richrath Memorial Bench in East Peoria, Illinois. Fans from the Remembering Gary Richrath Facebook group raised funds and navigated permits to install the golden-colored bench at River Front Park along Riverside Drive in East Peoria, Illinois. (*Author*)

References

Billboard magazine – billboard.com
British Phonographic Industry – bpi.co.uk
Discogs Marketplace – discogs.com
The Great Hollywood Hangover – hollywoodhangover.com
Illinois Rock and Roll Museum – roadrock.org
Music Canada – musiccanada.com
Recording Industry Association of America – riaa.com
REO Speedwagon – reospeedwagon.com
Arnie White – www.arniewhite.com

Interviews:

Boulanger, Eric (phone) 16 Jun 2022
Conroy, Carolyn: (phone) 2 Mar 2022
Claar Flom, Nancy: (email) 11 Feb 2022
Gleicher, Marvin: (email) 1 Feb 2022, 3 Feb 2022
Habeck, Ted (email) 3 May 2022
Jahnz, Michael (phone) 21 Mar 2022, (in person) 3 Jun 2022
Lear, Graham (phone) 17Mar 2022
Luttrell, Terry (in person) 29 May 2022
Scorfina, Steve: (phone) 2 Feb 2022
Scott, Jimmy (email) 6 May 2022
Shepard, Marty: (email) 3 Feb 2022, (phone) 4 Feb 2022
Volz, Greg X.: (email) 15 Feb 2022
White, Arnie: (email) 13 Feb 2022